Translated Texts for
Volume 19

MW01259790

Caesarius of Arles:
Life, Testament, Letters

Translated with notes and introduction by
WILLIAM E. KLINGSHIRN

Liverpool
University
Press

First published 1994 by
Liverpool University Press
PO Box 147, Liverpool, L69 3BX

British Library Cataloguing-in-Publication Data
A British Library CIP Record is available
ISBN 0 85323 368 3

Printed in the European Community by
Bell & Bain Limited, Glasgow

CONIUGI
DULCISSIMAE

CONTENTS

ACKNOWLEDGMENTS

It is a pleasure to thank those who have helped in the preparation of this volume, especially Margaret Gibson and Robert Markus, who first proposed the project and helped to see it through; Raymond Van Dam, who read the entire work and offered helpful advice throughout; and Frank Mantello, whose familiarity with later Latin prose saved me from many an infelicity. I am also grateful to Cynthia White for help in obtaining research materials, to William McCarthy for computer advice, and to Georgetta Cooper and Caitlyn Gilhooly for cartographic assistance.

In addition, I would like to acknowledge the generous financial assistance of the National Endowment for the Humanities, the Woodrow Wilson National Fellowship Foundation, and the Mrs. Giles Whiting Foundation. Their support for the research on Caesarius in which this volume shares was instrumental in its completion.

My final and greatest debt of gratitude is to my wife Patricia, to whom I have dedicated this book. For her keen interest in Caesarius and advice and encouragement throughout the project I am inexpressibly grateful.

ABBREVIATIONS

CCSL	*Corpus Christianorum, Series Latina*
CIL	*Corpus Inscriptionum Latinarum*
CSEL	*Corpus Scriptorum Latinorum Ecclesiasticorum*
CTh	*Codex Theodosianus*, ed. T. Mommsen and P. M. Meyer, *Theodosiani Libri XVI*, 2nd ed., I (Berlin, 1954)
Duchesne	L. Duchesne, *Fastes épiscopaux de l'ancienne Gaule*, 2nd ed., 3 vols. (Paris, 1907–15)
Krusch	*Vita Caesarii Episcopi Arelatensis*, ed. B. Krusch, *MGH SRM* 3, 433–501
MGH AA	*Monumenta Germaniae Historica, Auctores Antiquissimi*
MGH Ep.	*Monumenta Germaniae Historica, Epistolae*
MGH SRM	*Monumenta Germaniae Historica, Scriptores Rerum Merovingicarum*
Morin	*Sancti Caesarii episcopi Arelatensis Opera omnia nunc primum in unum collecta*, ed. G. Morin, I: *Sermones* (Maredsous, 1937); II: *Opera Varia* (Maredsous, 1942)
NPNF	A Select Library of the Nicene and post-Nicene Fathers of the Christian Church, ed. P. Schaff and H. Wace (New York, 1890–1900)
PL	*Patrologia Latina*
PLRE	A. H. M. Jones et al., *Prosopography of the Later Roman Empire*, 3 vols. (Cambridge, 1971–92)
SC	*Sources chrétiennes*
Schanz–Hosius	M. Schanz, C. Hosius, and G. Krüger, *Geschichte der römischen Litteratur*, IV. 2 (Munich, 1920)
Thiel	A. Thiel, *Epistolae romanorum pontificum genuinae et quae ad eos scriptae sunt a s. Hilaro usque ad Pelagium II* (Braunsberg, 1867)
TLL	*Thesaurus Linguae Latinae*
TTH	*Translated Texts for Historians*

de Vogüé–
Courreau

A. de Vogüé and J. Courreau, *Césaire d'Arles.*
Œuvres monastiques, I: *Œuvres pour les moniales*,
SC 345 (Paris, 1988)

GENERAL INTRODUCTION

THE CAREER OF CAESARIUS

When Caesarius became bishop of Arles in December 502, he reached the apex of an already successful ecclesiastical career.[1] Born in 469/70 to a wealthy Gallo-Roman family in the territory of Chalon-sur-Saône, he entered the local clergy at the age of seventeen. Two years later he left Chalon to become a monk on the renowned island of Lérins. After several years at Lérins, Caesarius was sent to Arles by his abbot to recover his health, which he had reportedly ruined by excessive mortification. He was warmly received in Arles by his close relation bishop Aeonius, who ordained him deacon and priest, and in 499 made him abbot of the men's monastery in Arles. Aeonius's final act of patronage on behalf of his young relative was to designate him as his successor. When Aeonius died in 501/2, Caesarius succeeded him as bishop, although not without considerable opposition from the local clergy, many of whom resented the rapid promotion of an outsider over more qualified local candidates. Despite numerous attempts by his clergy to depose him, he remained bishop of Arles until his death on 27 August 542.[2]

This was not a particularly unusual career for a pious and ambitious aristocrat in late antique Gaul. Already during the fifth century the episcopate had become an office for which Gallo-Roman aristocrats believed it was worthwhile to compete.[3] As Gaul increasingly came under the control of Franks, Burgundians, and Visigoths during the fifth century, opportunities for imperial careers were diminished. Aristocrats began to turn to the episcopate in increasing numbers to continue family traditions of office-holding, patronage, and public service. At the same time, the Roman (and by now largely Christian) cities of Gaul, which had always been in need of aristocratic benefactors and patrons, eagerly sought the assistance of local aristocrats—often in their capacity as bishops—to promote their prosperity, protect them in times of war,

---

[1] The standard biographies of Caesarius are Arnold (1894) and Malnory (1894). Also very useful is Delage (1971–86) I, 13–216. For further commentary on many points raised in this volume, see Klingshirn (1994).

[2] On the dates of Caesarius's episcopacy, see Klingshirn (1992).

[3] Griffe (1964–6) II, 213–35.

famine, and political disorder, and represent their interests before barbarian kings and nobles. That an aristocrat like Caesarius had arrived at his episcopal see by way of a monastery rather than from the ranks of the local clergy or directly from the laity was also not unusual. Many future bishops had lived for a time in monasteries, often as abbots, and the monastery at Lérins was especially renowned as a source of bishops.

THE DIOCESE OF ARLES

The diocese over which Caesarius presided as bishop was coterminous with an administrative district (*civitas*) created by the Romans, whose capital was located at Arles.[4] It consisted of the walled city of Arles, its immediate suburbs, and an extensive hinterland, which itself contained smaller towns, villages, and villas, many of which also served by the early sixth century as parish centers. The great majority of the population of the diocese lived in these smaller settlements rather than in the walled city or its suburbs, and made a living through agriculture, animal herding, and small-scale trading and manufacturing. The residents of the city and suburbs of Arles owed their livelihood to the city's role as an administrative center, river port, market for food and manufactured articles, collection point for taxes and rents, and episcopal see—all of which were made possible by its strategic location at the first landing place for ships sailing up the Rhône and the closest point to the sea for bridging the river.

A Roman city of moderate importance since the first century BC, Arles attained a new prominence at the beginning of the fourth century AD when the emperor Constantine the Great established an imperial residence and a mint in the city. Around 395 the city gained further in importance when the emperor Honorius moved the headquarters of the praetorian prefect of Gaul from Trier to Arles to protect it from barbarian attack. The bishops of Arles soon attempted to raise the city's ecclesiastical status to correspond to its enhanced civil status.[5] By 450, with the help of a favorable ruling by pope Leo, they succeeded in winning metropolitan control over an extensive ecclesiastical province. Depending on the location of civil boundaries and the relative strength

---

[4] A cultural geography of the *civitas* of Arles is available in Rivet (1988), 190–211.
[5] For an account of their efforts, see Mathisen (1989).

of the rival metropolitan bishops, its exact size fluctuated over the years (*Letter* 6). As metropolitan, the bishop of Arles was responsible for convening councils of his suffragan bishops, supervising the ordination of new suffragan bishops, and overseeing the affairs of the dioceses that made up his ecclesiastical province.

In 476/7 the Visigothic king Euric completed his conquest of southern Gaul by annexing the territory between the Rhône and the Durance. With this event Arles passed permanently out of the control of the Roman empire. The city remained in Visigothic hands until 508 when it was rescued from a Burgundian and Frankish siege by an army of the Ostrogothic king Theoderic, who promptly re-established the praetorian prefecture that the Visigoths had abolished. In 536, to free up their forces for war against Justinian and to protect their western flank, Theoderic's successors ceded the city and the rest of Provence to the Franks, who controlled it thereafter.[6]

CAESARIUS AS BISHOP

Caesarius is chiefly depicted in the *Life* as a monk, a reformer, a miracle-worker, and above all a deeply "pastoral" bishop.[7] His monastic sympathies are evident not just in his activities as a monk at Lérins and abbot in Arles, but also in his work as a bishop, particularly in his foundation of the first women's monastery in Arles, his composition of monastic rules for both of the city's monasteries, and his adherence to an ascetic style of life. His work as a reformer in the Gallic church was influenced by his own training as monk and by a contemporary movement of ecclesiastical reform, which included his own teacher, Julianus Pomerius.[8] Drawing his inspiration from the life and writings of Augustine of Hippo, Pomerius insisted that bishops and their clergy should live more like monks and less like aristocrats. In particular, he condemned the luxurious, worldly, and acquisitive habits of life in which the clergy indulged—for instance, feasting at lavish banquets, training hawks and hounds for the hunt, enlarging their estates, and enjoying "secular" learning— and urged bishops instead to give away their

[6] Wolfram (1988), 188–9, 309, 343–4.
[7] See Griffe (1980), and Beck (1950), which is largely a history of Caesarius's pastoral efforts.
[8] Ladner (1959), 389–90, and Klingshirn (1994), 75–82.

personal wealth, eat and dress simply, delegate the management of ecclesiastical property to subordinates, and live a life of asceticism in
common with their clergy.[9] Moreover, instead of neglecting the spiritual needs of their congregations to look after their own interests, bishops were urged to instruct the congregation by furnishing a good example and preaching regularly, not in the elegant rhetoric that only aristocrats could understand, but in a clear and simple style accessible to
all.[10]

By taking up this advice within his own diocese and by encourag-
ing similar behavior among his suffragan bishops, Caesarius identified
himself with this movement of church reform and became its most in-
fluential spokesman. Having already renounced his family inheritance
and given away the bulk of his personal property, he entered the episcopate of Arles with essentially no wealth of his own, and kept very little
of what he was subsequently given: when he died forty years later he
left an estate consisting of only two slaves and a few items of clothing
(Testament). Moreover, following the advice of Augustine, Pomerius,
and others, he also spurned the use of silver at his table (Life I. 37), rejected secular learning (Life I. 9), shunned comfortable clothing (Life II.
42), delegated the management of church lands to deacons (Life I. 15),
and organized a group of his urban clergy into a monastic community
(Life II. 6, 31–4).

Above all, Caesarius conceived of his role as a pastor in reformist
and monastic terms. He encouraged his urban and rural congregations
to pray frequently, to read the Bible regularly, to attend services in the
cathedral, to give away their possessions in the form of alms and tithes,
and as far as possible to adhere to monastic standards of personal behavior. To overcome widespread opposition from his congregation to the
Christian system of values, beliefs, and practices he advocated,
Caesarius turned to preaching. As his corpus of over 250 surviving
sermons demonstrates, he preached vividly, passionately, and simply—
in a Latin style far more accessible to the "unsophisticated and simple
people" in his audience (Sermon 86. 1) than the elegant rhetoric of
other aristocratic bishops.[11] He extended these efforts by authorizing
the priests and deacons in his rural parishes to preach in his absence

---

[9] De vita contemplativa I. 8, 13, 15; II. 9, 11, 16; III. 17.
[10] Ibid. I. 23.
[11] Auerbach (1965), 85–112.

(*Life* I. 54). He also tried to communicate his message by non-verbal means, for instance, by exemplary public behavior, impressive religious ceremonies, and ritual acts of healing and exorcism.

Caesarius used his position as metropolitan of the province of Arles to spread these ideas and practices beyond his own diocese. He sent letters to his fellow bishops (for instance, the encyclical letter published as *Serm.* 1), advocated reforms at the councils of Agde (506), Arles (524), Carpentras (527), and Vaison (529), and distributed collections of his sermons to visiting clergy. In addition, as Morin has argued, he is likely to have written as many as four theological treatises about grace, the Trinity, the Arian heresy, and the Book of Revelation.[12] His most important theological accomplishment was the forging of a compromise at the council of Orange in 529 on the issue of grace and free will, which put an end to the so-called "semi-Pelagian" controversy.[13]

Although only a fraction of it survives, Caesarius's correspondence with his fellow aristocrats and bishops in Gaul and Italy hints at close connections with the wider world beyond the diocese and province of Arles. He maintained a particularly close relationship with the bishops of Rome, who supported his claims to regional hegemony in return for his acknowledgment of their claims to universal primacy. This relationship was institutionalized by Pope Symmachus (498–514) who in 513 made Caesarius "papal vicar" of Gaul with the responsibility of overseeing papal interests in the region (*Letters* 7b, 8b). It was a responsibility he carried out with a limited degree of success, as the correspondence shows. But if nothing else, his connection with Rome provided him with an important source of outside support for reform at a time when support within his province may have been less than enthusiastic.

Caesarius's reform ideas and practices were not widely promoted by the Merovingian church after his death. No Merovingian council, for instance, restated the reform provisions of the councils of Carpentras (527) and Vaison (529), which had sought to promote rural parishes as centers of christianization by increasing the autonomy of their clergy. Caesarius's work was not rejected or forgotten, however. The canons of his councils continued to be included in conciliar collections, and his

[12] These are edited in Morin II, 159–277.
[13] Markus (1989).

sermons continued to be copied and distributed. Eventually it was such documents as these that formed the basis for a comprehensive effort under the Carolingians in the late eighth and early ninth centuries to reform the Frankish church.[14]

The documents translated here illuminate the historical context within which Caesarius's activities as a monk, a pastor, and a reformer took place and laid the foundation for his future influence. Studied side by side with his monastic rules, sermons, and councils, they not only provide a portrait of Caesarius's achievements, but also supply an important complement to the picture of sixth-century Gaul that emerges from the pages of Gregory of Tours. Caesarius's Gaul was both more Roman and more Mediterranean than Gregory's Gaul. It was in regular communication with Rome and the East, and enjoyed the distant toleration of Arian Goths rather than the intrusive proximity of catholic Franks. Above all, influenced more by the spirituality of Lérins than by the cult of St. Martin, its ideals of christianization gave as much weight to the power of rhetoric as to the potency of relics. The transformation of late Roman Gaul into early medieval France, and in particular, the ways in which local communities began to identify themselves as Christian and Christianity itself was remade into a community religion, suggest a process of very considerable complexity. By supplying important evidence from a local context and a set of preoccupations significantly different from those of Gregory of Tours, Caesarius's career and writings can help us to better reconstruct and so understand that complexity.

THE TRANSLATIONS

"Everything suffers by translation except a bishop" according to the old saying. This includes, we might add, writings by and about a bishop. Late Latin prose presents special difficulties for the translator. Its fondness for florid description, abstract expression, and highly rhetorical language, which conveyed a sense of formality and elegance to late antique audiences, often seems pompous and overwrought to modern readers. In seeking to produce an accurate and readable English translation of these writings, I have found it necessary to alter or elimi-

[14] McKitterick (1977).

nate some characteristic features of late Latin style, such as verbal redundancies and multiple superlatives. Other features I have decided to retain, for instance deferential periphrases for the second person such as "your brotherhood" and "your charity."[15] These expressions not only convey the self-consciously hierarchical framework in which aristocrats situated one another and themselves, but also reveal the immense effort they devoted to masking and managing their mutual disagreements.[16] In general, I have tried to remain as close as possible to what I think the authors of these texts were trying to say. Although I have generally modernized place names where they can be identified, I have not done so with the names of individuals, unless their modern equivalents are either so familiar (Augustine) or so common (Peter) that retaining ancient versions would have seemed pedantic. Translations of verses from the Latin Bible are my own, and references are made to the Revised Standard Version rather than the Vulgate, as in Morin's text. Editorial comments and supplements to the text are enclosed in square brackets, and suspected interpolations in double square brackets.

---

[15] A full survey can be found in O'Brien (1930).

[16] I owe this point to Raymond Van Dam.

THE LIFE OF CAESARIUS

INTRODUCTION

COMPOSITION

The two books of the *Life of Caesarius* were composed within seven years of the bishop's death by five clerics of his acquaintance. The architect of the work as a whole and the principal author of Book I was Cyprianus, a close associate of Caesarius who served as bishop of Toulon from *c*.517 to *c*.545.[1] He was assisted in the composition of Book I by two other bishops, listed in order of seniority in the prologue to Book I. Firminus served as bishop of Uzès from *c*.534 to *c*.552. He may have been related to the Firminus of *Life* I. 8.[2] Viventius, whose see is uncertain, served from *c*.541 to sometime before 549.[3] Book II in turn was composed by two diocesan clerics who had attended Caesarius since their adolescence. Messianus, a priest, had served as a notary (*Life* I. 40; II. 8) and a letter carrier (*Letter* 8a), and Stephanus, a deacon, resided with other clerics in the bishop's house (*Life* II. 5–6).

The *Life* was organized to take advantage of the particular interests and capacities of its authors, who had acquired different kinds of knowledge about Caesarius on the basis of their different ecclesiastical ranks and duties. The authors of Book I, who knew Caesarius as a bishop and metropolitan, concentrated on his "life and way of life" (I. 1). After a brief prologue (I. 1–2), they discussed, in largely chronological order, Caesarius's birth, adolescence, and monastic career, his ordination as bishop, his pastoral work in the diocese, his travels outside the diocese, and his diplomatic relations with barbarian kings and fellow bishops. The latest datable events in this narrative are the council of Orange

---

[1] Fusconi (1963).

[2] Viard (1964).

[3] Viventius's name first appears on the signature list of the council of Orléans in 541, *CCSL* 148A (1963), 143, line 53. Assuming that he was one of Caesarius's suffragan bishops, he could only have come from Cavaillon, Cimiez-Nice, Digne, or Riez, since these were the only dioceses not otherwise represented at the council. (Marseille can be ruled out, since its bishops traditionally refused to recognize Caesarius's metropolitan authority.) Whatever Viventius's diocese, since all of these sees sent representatives to the council of Orléans in 549, he had probably died by that year.

(529) and pope Boniface's letter of 531 (I. 60). Contained within this chronological structure, and subordinated to it, are various sections organized by topic (I. 45–55, 61–2) which discuss the bishop's habits, character, and miracles. The book ends with a brief conclusion (I. 63), which introduces the narrative of Messianus and Stephanus, who were asked to supplement the account of Caesarius in Book I with their own knowledge, in much the same way as the characters in Sulpicius Severus's *Dialogi* were asked to add to the *Vita Martini* what they knew of the bishop.[4]

In response to this request, the authors of Book II, who knew Caesarius as a teacher and a superior, decided to focus on his "way of life and miracles" (II. 1). Their narrative can be divided into three parts, the first two organized topically and the last organized chronologically. In the first part, after a brief prologue (II. 1), Messianus and Stephanus discussed Caesarius's daily routine, his travels within the diocese, his spirituality, and numerous incidents of healing and exorcism (II. 2–36). Their contribution to the *Life* seems to have originally ended at this point, since a brief peroration follows (II. 37). In the second part of the book, an account was given of the posthumous miracles attributed to Caesarius's relics (II. 38–44). In the third part, the chronological order of Book I was resumed, near the point at which it had left off, with the Frankish takeover of Arles in 536 (II. 45). After a brief panegyric of the Frankish king Childebert, Caesarius's last days, death, and burial were discussed (II. 45–50). Thus despite its division into separate sections, some chronologically and others topically organized, the work as a whole stands as a single chronological structure, beginning with the birth of Caesarius in 469/70 (I. 3) and ending with his death and burial in 542 (II. 50).

While the collective contributions of the three authors of Book I and the two authors of Book II can be easily determined, their individual contributions to each book are more difficult to specify. It has been plausibly suggested that Cyprianus wrote the bulk of Book I himself, up to I. 58, since there is a first-person reference to him at I. 52 ("Woe to me, wretched Cyprianus"), an elegant compliment to Caesaria the Younger at I. 58 that recalls the prologue, and a brief encomium that he could not have written to himself at I. 60.[5] On this reckoning, it ap-

[4] Cavallin (1934), 25–6.
[5] Arnold (1894), 496.

pears that Firminus and Viventius composed I. 59–63, although it is impossible to assign individual chapters to each of them and, it must be said, also impossible to rule out the possibility that one or both of them contributed material to earlier chapters of Book I. Indeed, at least part of the narrative of Caesarius's journey to Italy (I. 37) is probably based on an account by Messianus, who accompanied Caesarius on his trip (I. 40).

Individual contributions to Book II are equally difficult to determine, but it is possible to make some suggestions. Many episodes are narrated in the first person singular (II. 5–6, 11, 13–15, 19, 20, 22, 27, 34, 38, 41, 42, 43, 44, 49), and in some of these the author's identity is revealed. It is clear, for instance, that Messianus wrote II. 22 and 27, since the author of these chapters identifies himself as Caesarius's notary.[6] Stephanus, in turn, probably wrote II. 5–6, 8–9, 13–15, and 33–4, since the author of these chapters appears to have been in a position to observe Caesarius's living, eating, and sleeping habits at close range; moreover, in II. 8–9 the narrator speaks of Messianus in the third person. Both authors probably took responsibility for the prologue and conclusions (II. 37, 50), since these sections are narrated in the first person plural. In addition, the insertion of the verbs *inquit* ("he said") and *dixerunt* ("they said") by Cyprianus or some other redactor at intervals throughout this section (II. 1, 11, 14, 22, 33)[7] makes it possible to suggest a tentative division of labor between Messianus and Stephanus for the whole of II. 1–37. If the final redactor of the *Life* inserted these words not only to cast Book II in dialogue form, as Cavallin suggested, but more particularly to indicate changes of speaker, then Messianus and Stephanus may have divided their work as follows:

II. 1	Messianus and Stephanus
II. 2–9	Stephanus
II. 10–12	Messianus
II. 13–21	Stephanus
II. 22–32	Messianus
II. 33–6	Stephanus
II. 37	Messianus and Stephanus

---

[6] Krusch, 452.
[7] Cavallin (1935–6), 14.

Unfortunately, such indications of authorship are lacking for II. 38–50.

FUNCTION

Cyprianus and his fellow clerics wrote the *Life of Caesarius* with a number of ends in mind. They claimed to have undertaken the project at the request of Caesaria the Younger, a close relation of Caesarius (possibly his niece), who served as abbess of the nunnery he had founded in Arles (I. 1). Although such claims were conventional in Latin prose prefaces,[8] the fact that the *Life of Caesarius* at least in part promoted the interests of the monastery suggests that Caesaria may actually have played a part in suggesting its composition. As a panegyric of the monastery's founder, the *Life* would have helped to enhance the prestige of the foundation. As an exemplary portrayal of the author of the monastery's rule—himself a dedicated ascetic—it would have provided the monastery's residents with an authoritative model for their own ascetic behavior. As a vivid recreation of the bishop's very presence (I. 1)—made all the more tangible by physical descriptions of his appearance and by repeated use of the present tense and direct quotations from his sermons and conversations—it would have brought the power of his sanctity and the potential for miracles into the very midst of its audience.[9] Thus, as a narrative of the holy man's past achievements and a conduit for his still-present spiritual power, it would have promoted the cult of Caesarius, and so encouraged support for the monastery that possessed his body, where the further performance of miracles could be expected.[10] It was precisely in such a context that passages from the *Life of Caesarius* were re-used in later *Lives* : Florentius's *Life* of Rusticula, who served as abbess of Caesarius's monastery from 574–632,[11] and Baudonivia's *Life* of Radegund, who used Caesarius's *Regula virginum* in the monastery she founded in Poitiers around the middle of the sixth century.[12] But the authors of the *Life of Caesarius* also wrote with a wider audience and a wider set of

[8] Janson (1964), 116–20.
[9] I am indebted to John Siman for a convincing demonstration of this point. See further Brown (1981), 80–5.
[10] For a more detailed discussion, see Klingshirn (1990), 464–74.
[11] Ed. B. Krusch, *MGH SRM* IV (1902), 337–51.
[12] Ed. B. Krusch, *MGH SRM* II (1888), 377–95.

purposes in mind. As admirers and supporters of Caesarius, they composed the *Life* to edify anyone who read or listened to the work (I. 2; II. 1), to celebrate their own association with the bishop, and to defend the bishop's reputation from attack by rivals. Above all, by portraying Caesarius as an ideal ascetic bishop, a widely admired holy man and miracle-worker, and an effective ecclesiastical reformer, they tried to promote after Caesarius's death the controversial reform ideas he had promoted all his life.

HISTORICAL VALUE

Like other saints' lives, the *Life of Caesarius* is a valuable source for the mental world of its authors and their immediate audience. For example, the abundance of miracle stories in the *Life* testifies not only to its contemporary use as an instrument for promoting the cult of St. Caesarius, but also to contemporary ideas of sanctity and the miraculous, which made such a use conceivable in the first place. Unlike many saints' lives, however, the *Life* also serves as a valuable source for the career of Caesarius and the times in which he lived. It was written soon after his death by men deeply familiar with his life, who claimed to draw their information from reliable sources: Caesarius himself, their own eyewitness observations, and the eyewitness observations of others (I. 1; II. 1). While such claims are a commonplace of hagiography, the *Life* itself largely substantiates them. Quotations from Caesarius's sermons (I. 18, 54, 61; II. 5, 6) and stories plausibly based on his own narration (I. 6, 29) can be identified throughout the work. Details supplied by one or another author are on many occasions of just the sort he was in a position to observe (I. 51; II. 6, 13–15, 19, 22). Reliance on the eyewitness testimony of others is confirmed in by the naming of informants (II. 10–12). Many of the events narrated in the *Life* can be corroborated by independent evidence.[13]

In addition to these sources, the authors of the *Life* also made use of oral traditions, which they heard at various places. The amusing and edifying story of Benenatus and his daughter, for instance, was told at the basilica of the Apostles in Arles (II. 24). These traditions were

---

[13] For example, Caesarius's exile in Bordeaux (I. 21) is also mentioned in a letter from Ruricius of Limoges (Caesarius, *Letter* 4); his trial before Theoderic (I. 36) is alluded to in a letter from Ennodius (Caesarius, *Letter* 1).

supplemented by stories modeled directly on the Bible (II. 13) and on earlier saints' lives, especially the *Life* of Caesarius's predecessor Hilarius (I. 27; II. 49–50; cf. *Vita Hilarii* 18, 28–29). Although the authors themselves were no doubt responsible for some of these borrowings, in other cases it might have been the actors themselves who modeled their behavior on biblical and patristic *exempla*.[14]

To be sure, even if based on the best of sources, the *Life* is still an avowedly polemical, partisan, and panegyrical work. But skepticism about its testimony should not be unfairly focused on any one element in the work. Miracles are a case in point.[15] The authors of the *Life* attribute many events to divine or miraculous causes, from rain showers at a time of drought to the expulsion of demons and the healing of the sick. Whatever doubts modern readers might have about such stories, there is little justification for treating them with more intensive critical scrutiny than other narratives in the *Life*, since they were based on the same sources and put into final written form by the same authors. It is likely, in fact, that stories of the "cures" worked by Caesarius as he traveled throughout his diocese were based on rituals he actually performed for the sick and possessed, such as we know he recommended in his sermons.[16] The same is true of healings attributed to Caesarius's relics, which depended on the widespread belief that privileged physical objects could conduct divine power. Not only do such narratives provide important evidence in themselves for religious actions and attitudes; their background details also supply valuable additional information. For instance, it is only from the account in Book II of Caesarius's travels throughout the countryside that we know the names of most of the parishes in the diocese of Arles. It is indeed a particular strength of Christian hagiography that it casts light on details of social life too humble for mention in other kinds of sources. True to form, the *Life of Caesarius* presents a series of memorable vignettes: peasants begging their landlord for relief from the Gothic soldiers who trampled their fields while hunting wild boar (I. 48), a bishop wedging himself into the narrow space between a bed and bedside chest in the room where a teenage girl lay ill (II. 2), and a Frank asking in agonizingly bad Latin for relics to cure his fever (II. 42). At the same time, the *Life*

[14] Scheibelreiter (1983), 136–7.
[15] See McCready (1989), 111–75.
[16] *Serm.* 13. 3; 19. 5; 50. 1; 184. 5. See Klingshirn (1994), 159–70.

also casts light on the wider history of Arles and Provence at a time of deep political instability. It furnishes valuable details about the barbarian government of Arles, its local aristocracy, Jewish-Christian relations within the city, and the impact of the war of 507/9 on Provence. Without the *Life of Caesarius*, our knowledge of religion and society in early sixth-century Provence would be far poorer.

TEXT AND TRANSLATION

The authors of both books of the *Life* apologized to their readers and listeners for the "rusticity" of their diction, grammar, and style (I. 2; II. 1, 37, 43), but insisted at the same time that their religious intentions and the simplicity of their audience demanded an "unadorned" style, "the eloquence of fishermen rather than rhetoricians" (I. 2). This was of course a hagiographical commonplace, and although the *Life* as a whole was not as ornate, mannered, or classically "correct" as other contemporary hagiographical writings, such as Ennodius's *Life of Epiphanius*, it can hardly be said to have been written in an "unadorned" style, let alone in the language of fishermen or peasants. In fact, the *Life of Caesarius* was written in the ordinary Latin of educated persons in early sixth-century Gaul. In Book I, for instance, the rhythmic endings of clauses (known as *clausulae*) have been shown to follow typical patterns of early sixth-century Latin prose.[17] Moreover, the orthography, syntax, and diction of both books,[18] as well as their use of rhetorical figures like pleonasm and parallelism,[19] are typical of later Latin. Where they exist, differences between the language and style of Books I and II generally correspond to differences between the social standing and education of their respective authors. Not surprisingly, Book II is on the whole less well written than Book I, but neither book is without its share of awkward phrases and clumsy expressions. At the same time, there are passages of vivid and moving prose in both books.

This translation is based on Morin's edition of 1942, which in turn largely depends on Cavallin's modifications to Krusch's edition of 1896. Cavallin's principal contribution was to demonstrate that the eleventh-century manuscript on which Krusch relied heavily (*codex*

---

[17] Cavallin (1948), 143–8.
[18] Cavallin (1934).
[19] Sticca (1954), 98–104.

Paris., B. N. lat. 5295) represented a less faithful version of the archetype than previously believed since, among other lapses, its learned copyist corrected much of the "incorrect" Merovingian spelling and syntax of the original, and interpolated a number of passages into the text.[20] Although he did not produce a new edition of the *Life* himself, Cavallin did provide the materials for doing so, which Morin largely accepted into his own edition. In addition to these studies, Cavallin provided a concordance to Krusch's text of the *Life of Caesarius* in his edition of the *Lives* of Honoratus and Hilarius.[21] Along with their value for the text, Cavallin's studies of the *Life* provide a useful commentary on the language of the work and the meaning of disputed passages, and I have relied extensively upon them. I have also profited from J. N. Hillgarth's English translation of selections from Book I of the *Life of Caesarius.*[22]

---

[20] Cavallin (1934), 35–7.
[21] Cavallin (1952), 118–99.
[22] Hillgarth (1986), 32–43.

THE LIFE OF CAESARIUS
BOOK I

Here begins the Prologue to the Life of the holy Caesarius, written by
the bishops lord Cyprianus, blessed Firminus, and holy Viventius,
and by the priest Messianus and the deacon Stephanus.

1. You, Caesaria, whom we honor as a virgin, together with the
choir of fellow nuns entrusted to you, have been asking that we fulfill
our obligation to recall and to write an account from the very beginning
of the life and way of life of your founder, St. Caesarius of blessed
memory. He now enjoys the reward of that life because of his way of
life, whose blessedness cannot be expressed in human speech.
Although some time ago, while he was living here, his life was reverently made known throughout the whole world, we consider it wrong
not to comply with so holy a request, especially since this work can
stand in place of his presence for your—and even more his—monastery.
And when we speak of him, we rejoice because in a certain sense we
also see him. With God's help then we shall try to fulfill your request.
Many facts we have ascertained from the statements of our most blessed
master himself. Many occurrences we have seen with our own eyes.
And some details we have learned from the accounts of the venerable
priests and deacons who are his disciples, but especially by the venerable priest Messianus and the most faithful deacon Stephanus, both of
whom served him from youth. We have included only as much as
would not seem burdensome or prolix.

2. In this dedication of our little work, we ask our readers for one
indulgence, that if it should happen that we, as simple narrators, attract
the attention and judgments of scholars, they not criticize us on the
grounds that our style lacks ornate diction and correct grammar.[1] For
the light of Caesarius's works and the ornaments of his virtues are sufficient for us, who truthfully relate the actions, words, and merits of so
great a man. Indeed, the renowned lord Caesarius, whom we know in

---

[1] Apologies for stylistic and grammatical deficiencies are common in prologues to the Latin saints' lives. For an analysis of these prologues, see
Strunk (1970), esp. 52–3, 74–6. On apologies for defective style in Latin
prose prefaces generally, see Janson (1964), 124–41.

his work, used to say, "Some avoid rusticity of speech but do not turn aside from the vices of life." For the unadorned righteousness of the virgins of Christ deserves that nothing embellished[2] and nothing arranged with worldly skill be offered to please their eyes or ears. They should rather take up the words of the most unadorned of narratives flowing from the fountain of simple truth. Content therefore with a religious innocence, our style has renounced worldly ostentation, because it has rejected the boasting of worldly glory and its works. It delights instead in imitating the eloquence of fishermen rather than of rhetoricians.[3] Now then let each seek to follow in his life what he hastens to learn by reading.

Here ends the Prologue and begins the Life
of the same holy and most blessed bishop.

3. The holy and most blessed Caesarius, bishop of Arles, was a native of the territory of Chalon-sur-Saône.[4] His parents as well as his family—an exceptionally great example of honor and nobility—were distinguished above all their fellow citizens because of their faith and even more their conduct. When he was seven years old or a little older, the holy and venerable Caesarius never hesitated to make gifts to the poor of the garments he wore. Often, when the blessed man had been seen by his parents returning home half naked, and was questioned under threat of punishment about what he had done with his clothes, he would only respond that they had been carried off by passersby.

4. And so, just as small trees are sometimes accustomed to bear fruit from noble shoots before growing up, and the younger they are, the more pleasing is their fruitfulness, so in that holy man, during the very beginnings of his infancy, the happy offshoot of flourishing hope burst forth, with the result that before he blossomed in age, he abounded in the fruit of character. In his eighteenth year [486/7], without the knowledge of his household or parents, he first offered supplica-

---

[2] Literally, "painted" or "dyed"; cf. *Regula virginum* 44, 45, a reference I owe to Conrad Leyser.
[3] For a history of this widespread *topos*, see Bambeck (1983).
[4] A prosperous river port in late antiquity, Chalon was by the time of Caesarius's birth probably controlled by the Burgundians, who had been settled in eastern Gaul as federates in *c*.442, James (1982), 21–4.

tion and then prostrated himself at the feet of holy Silvester, because he wished to reside in the heavenly kingdom.[5] He asked that, once he had been tonsured and had put on a habit, the bishop deliver him up into divine service and not permit a suppliant to be called back later by his parents to the family estate and his former attachments. The bishop then thanked Christ, and there was no delay in fulfilling these marvelous vows. And when, after this beginning, Caesarius had served there for two or more years, he was set aflame by the promptings of divine grace and decided to bind himself more closely and with fewer impediments to divine service, in accordance with the gospel, so that, out of love for the heavenly kingdom, he might become a stranger not only to his parents, but also to his homeland.

5. And so, when he had taken the opportunity of fleeing for his salvation from the shackles of the world, the holy recruit sought the monastery of Lérins [488/9].[6] While *en route*, accompanied by only a single slave, he crossed a river in the vicinity of a search party sent by his mother, but they did not see him. The devil, however, followed him in the form of a poor man he had possessed, who called out repeatedly behind him, "Caesarius, do not go!" Caesarius at once cured this man by blessing a cup and offering it to him to drink. Knowledge of this event came from the testimony of Caesarius's previously mentioned companion; it is agreed that this was Caesarius's first miracle. He was then admitted [into the monastery] by the holy abbot Porcarius and by all the senior monks.[7] He began to be well-disposed at vigils, attentive in observation, quick in obedience, dedicated to work, distinguished in humility, and remarkable in gentleness. As a result, the

[5] Silvester was bishop of Chalon from c.485 to c.527, Duchesne II, 193. He took part in the councils of Epaone (517) and Lyon (518/23). The healing powers of his bed are related in Gregory of Tours, *In gloria confessorum* 84.

[6] Located on a small island in the Mediterranean not far from Cannes, the monastery had been founded between 400 and 410 by Honoratus, later bishop of Arles. It grew to become the most famous monastery in late antique Provence. The story of its foundation is related in Hilarius of Arles, *Vita Honorati* 15–17. For its history in the fifth century, see Pricoco (1978).

[7] Apart from the *Life*, Porcarius is known only as the author of the *Monita*, a brief treatise on monastic life, ed. Wilmart (1909).

monks rejoiced to discover that he whom they had received for instruction in the rudiments of the discipline of the rule had already been made perfect in the advanced principles of the whole teaching.[8]

6. After a short while he was chosen cellarer of the community.[9] Carefully and enthusiastically he began to make disbursements to those in need, even if out of love of abstinence they asked for nothing. But to those he had shown not to be in need, he did not distribute anything, however much they wanted to receive something. For this reason those who were hostile to Caesarius's holy discrimination petitioned the abbot to remove him from the office of cellarer. This was done. Soon after he had put aside this duty, Caesarius so afflicted himself by his constant desire for reading, singing psalms, praying, and keeping vigils that finally, by an excess of asceticism, he brought it about that his feeble young body, which should properly have been coddled rather than weakened, was bent and broken. For example, he drew a week's nourishment from a meager concoction of vegetables and gruel, which he used to prepare for himself on Sundays.[10]

7. These good deeds, therefore, shone out among the first of his merits, and later in life they were increased by many miracles. For he wore down the robustness of his flesh, so that he might firm up the power of his spirit by the solidity of hope and faith. And, as the apostle says, triumphing over his very self [cf. Col. 2: 15], so that in complete victory he might deserve to be crowned, he transferred exterior qualities to the possession of the "inner man" [Rom. 7: 22] and cast away the rebellious urgings of his body by the commands of his splendid mind. After this however, when his stomach began to fail, he developed a quartan fever. The holy abbot Porcarius was gravely disturbed by Caesarius's illness, and the sickness was shared between master and pupil in such a way that the former suffered in spirit and the latter in

[8] It is possible that the *Regula Macarii*, an extant rule of uncertain provenance, was the rule in effect during Caesarius's sojourn at Lérins, de Vogüé (1982) II, 339–56.
[9] For a detailed description of the cellarer's responsibilities, see *Regula Benedicti* 31.
[10] Evidently, Caesarius ate only once a week, a practice common to the desert fathers of Egypt, but rejected by Cassian as too harsh for Gallic monks, *De institutis coenobiorum* V. 23.

body. The holy father saw that no remedy could be furnished to him in the monastery, for even if a physician had been present there, the young man's routine permitted him no relaxation at all from the reins of abstinence or the rigor of vigils, burning as he was with a desire for spiritual things. The most holy abbot therefore ordered Caesarius—indeed, forced him—to be taken to Arles to regain his health.[11]

8. There were at that time in Arles two individuals whose zeal, vigilance, and concern for clerics and monks as well as for citizens and the poor made their city even more renowned: the illustrious Firminus,[12] a devout Christian, and his relative Gregoria, a most noble matron and the most illustrious of women.[13] Neither of them spent their wealth on worldly luxury; instead, they transferred their resources to paradise for themselves by bringing relief to the poor. Out of mercy they welcomed holy Caesarius.

9. A man named Pomerius was very closely associated with Firminus and Gregoria.[14] He was a rhetorician by training and an African by birth, who had achieved distinction and fame there by teaching the art of grammar. Seeing that the holy Caesarius was remarkably full of God's grace, and was endowed by the gift of Christ with a wonderfully retentive memory,[15] these noble-spirited individuals conceived the idea that his monastic simplicity should be refined by the teachings

[11] Arles was well known for its physicians. See Caesarius, *Letter* 2, and Arnold (1894), 66–7.
[12] This aristocrat is probably the same Firminus who corresponded with Sidonius Apollinaris c.480 (*Epist.* IX. 1 and 16) and with Magnus Felix Ennodius in 502/3 (*Epist.* I. 8 and II. 7). His title indicates that he belonged to the highest rank of the aristocracy, Jones (1964) I, 528–30. See further *PLRE* II, 471 (Firminus 4).
[13] Gregoria is known only from this passage. She may have been Firminus's wife. See *PLRE* II, 520.
[14] Julianus Pomerius fled Africa in the wake of Vandal persecution and settled in Arles in the late fifth century, where he was ordained a priest. His most important surviving work, *De vita contemplativa*, was a pastoral handbook for bishops. For his career and writings, see Suelzer (1947), 3–12, and Solignac (1974).
[15] Faculties of memory were much esteemed in antiquity. For an illuminating discussion of the moral and creative uses of memory, see Carruthers (1990).

of worldly knowledge. But he whom[16] divine grace had prepared to be instructed for and through itself did not accept the inventions of human learning. So it happened one day that when he had grown weary from a vigil, he placed on his bed under his shoulder the book that his teacher had given him to read. When he had fallen asleep on it, he was soon struck with a terrible vision of divine inspiration. During his brief nap, he saw the shoulder on which he was lying and the arm with which he had been resting on the book being gnawed by a serpent winding itself around him. Terrified by what he had seen, he was shaken out of his sleep and he began to blame himself more severely for wanting to join the light of the rule of salvation to the foolish wisdom of the world. And so he at once condemned these preoccupations, for he knew that those endowed with spiritual understanding possessed the adornment of perfect eloquence.

10. Several days later Firminus and Gregoria made a suggestion to the holy Aeonius, bishop of the city.[17] They said that a monk worthy of respect and outstanding in every virtue was staying in their house, and that the bishop ought to meet and become acquainted with him in a private interview. Aeonius therefore ordered Caesarius to be introduced to him. When holy Caesarius had been presented to him, the venerable bishop Aeonius questioned him carefully about his native city and his parents. And when Caesarius had announced the name of the city and the lineage of his parents, the bishop immediately rejoiced and said, "Son, you are my fellow citizen as well as my relative, for I remember your parents very well, and out of kinship I embrace you in memory of them." He then began to regard the young man not as a pilgrim or a foreigner but more warmly with the intimate eyes of the heart.

11. Soon bishop Aeonius asked his abbot, the holy Porcarius, to release him.[18] Because it was the blessed bishop Aeonius who made the request, Porcarius granted it, although reluctantly. Presently Caesarius was ordained deacon, then priest. Yet he never relinquished

[16] I have followed Krusch, who reads *quem*, rather than Morin, who reads *quam*.
[17] Aeonius was bishop of Arles from c.485 to 501/2, Duchesne I, 257.
[18] This act of courtesy would later be required by church law, Agde (506), can. 27, *CCSL* 148 (1963), 205.

the canonical regularity of a monk or the practices of Lérins, not even slightly. Though a cleric in rank and office, he remained a monk in humility, charity, obedience, and asceticism. At Matins and other services he was the first to enter the church and the last to depart. Neither what he saw nor what he heard distracted the attention of the blessed man from the nectar of celestial blessings, with the result that his expression always seemed to shine forth like something heavenly.

12. Then the abbot on a suburban island of the city died [498/9].[19] The holy Aeonius directed the blessed father Caesarius to succeed with the same revered authority and to govern with an abbot's discipline the monastery that had recently been abandoned by its leader. He willingly took up a life in the suburban monastery that he always cultivated by his daily actions even within the city and that he always hoped for in his prayers. And through daily perseverance and the divine office he organized the monastery so well that it is preserved there even today, God willing.

13. Now when Caesarius had spent a little over three years on the island as abbot, holy Aeonius addressed the clergy and citizens, and through messengers asked the [Visigothic] masters of the city[20] that after he had departed, God willing, to Christ they choose none other than holy Caesarius to succeed him. He made this request so that the community might rejoice at the prospect that Caesarius, the servant of Christ, would restore the discipline of the church, which Aeonius always complained had been weakened in many of its rules by his ill health. Furthermore, Aeonius hoped that his successor's labor might constitute a benefit for himself, so that when he left such a successor, he might also obtain an increase in his eternal inheritance by the election of this most holy man. Finally he wished by the hope of this election to leave behind an ally after his death, who would also succeed him as a spokesman in dogma. And so, with all these things faithfully

[19] This island was probably the Ile de la Cappe, 3 km southeast of Arles, Février (1964), 70–1.
[20] For *ipsos dominos rerum* as Visigoths, see Krusch, 461, n. 3. Arles was at this time under the control of Alaric II, who had succeeded his father Euric at his death in 484. On Alaric's career and policies see Wolfram (1988), 190–202.

ordered by divine providence, and certain of his successor, the blessed
Aeonius departed to the Lord [16 August 501/2].[21]

14. Now when the reliable report that he was to be consecrated
bishop came to the notice of our father about whom we are speaking,
he tried to hide among some tombs. But he could not be hidden, for it
was divine grace and not his faults that revealed him. And so he was
dragged alive from one of the tombs, who was proved by the righteousness of his life to be not dead but hidden. Then under compulsion he
took up the burden of the episcopate and modestly bore the office that
was imposed on himself, a tamed beast of Christ [December 502].[22]

15. And so, as a prudent pastor who was concerned for the
progress of all, he immediately directed the clergy to sing every day in
the basilica of St. Stephen the offices of Terce, Sext, and None, in addition to hymns.[23] He did this so that if any layman or penitent wanted
to follow the holy office, he could be present at its daily celebration
without any excuse. Then in the fashion of the apostles he spurned all
anxiety and concern for the affairs of the world, and after calling upon
God as a witness he decided that responsibility for the management of
agriculture should be entrusted to managers and deacons.[24] He then
completely dedicated himself to the word of God, meditation, and constant preaching. In truth he was like a physician of the spirit, who
cured the innate vices of diseases and prevented new ones from arising
out of wicked thoughts.

[21] On the date of Aeonius's death see Klingshirn (1992), 85–6.

[22] For the ordination date see ibid., 84–5. The gap between Aeonius's death
and Caesarius's consecration suggests a contested election, Klingshirn
(1994), 84–7.

[23] The basilica of St. Stephen was the cathedral church of Arles. The addition of the canonical hours of Terce, Sext, and None to Matins and Vespers,
which were already celebrated in the cathedral, made the complete round of
monastic prayer available in the city, Beck (1950), 110–14.

[24] Augustine had taken a similar step (Possidius, *Vita Augustini* 24), which
Pomerius advised bishops in general to take (*De vita contemplativa* I. 8, 13.
1). The diocese of Arles, like other dioceses, owned substantial holdings in
land, whose revenues were used to support the clergy, furnish and repair
church buildings, and assist the poor. Cf. *Test.* 9.

16. God gave him so much skill in speaking about himself that whatever he could see with his eyes, he put forth in the reassuring form of analogies for the edification of his audience. He familiarized himself with a large collection of sacred volumes, but he always accumulated recent works in such a way that he lost none of the old. In this respect he greatly resembled the temple of God, which both welcomes new guests daily and cherishes the old, and always grows by the entrance of newcomers in such a way that it is never diminished by the departure of the old. And so, if circumstances demanded, he recited in succession countless *exempla* from the divine books. He did this as if he were reading what he knew out of a book, not as if he were drawing forth what he had once read from the storehouse of his memory. In this he fulfilled the gospel saying about the man who "draws forth from his storehouse things new and old" [Matt. 13: 52].

17. When bishops, priests, and all the members of the divine clergy came to see him, as well as citizens of Arles and even foreigners, Caesarius welcomed them, offered a prayer, and asked a few questions about the health and well-being of their fellow citizens and relatives. Soon, however, he took up the weapons of holy preaching. Discussing the impermanence of the present and proving the eternity of happiness, he motivated some with sweet speech and terrified others with sharper language. Some he corrected with threats, others with encouragement. Some he restrained from vices through love, others through threat of punishment. He warned some in a general sense through proverbs, and reproached others more harshly by calling on God as a witness. So that they would follow his warnings, he tearfully threatened them with eternal punishment. He preached in accordance with what he knew of each man's virtues, character, or vices, so that he might incite the good to glory and call back the wicked from punishment. Like a good physician he provided different remedies for different ailments; he did not offer what would please the patient, but rather what would cure him. He did not consider the wishes of the sick, but fittingly desired to heal the infirm.

18. He used to strongly reproach the holy bishops and other leaders of the church, so that they would provide spiritual nourishment unceasingly to the people entrusted to them.[25] "Brother, in the name of Christ," he said, "you occupy a position in the front rank of the spiritual army. Apply your pastoral expertise to the talents entrusted to you, so that you can restore them to the lender at double the value [cf. Matt. 25: 14–30]. Listen to the prophet: 'Woe to me, because I was silent!' [Isa. 6: 5]. Hear the apostle saying with fear: 'Woe to me if I do not spread the gospel' [1 Cor. 9: 16]. While you occupy a bishop's throne, see to it that no one is excluded, and that no one says to you: Those who were perhaps better able to serve the Lord's advancement 'have taken the key of knowledge, but they do not enter themselves, nor permit others to do so' [Luke 11: 52]." Through the Lord's inspiration he possessed this unique skill, that when he revealed details to individuals, he exposed to each person's eyes the course of his life. So all who heard him not only believed that Caesarius was an investigator of their hearts, but also acknowledged that he was a witness to their consciences. And just as Caesarius was very severe concerning himself, so he appeared strict in the correction of others.

19. In addition, he ordered the laity to learn psalms and hymns by heart and to sing sequences and antiphons in a loud and rhythmic voice like the clergy, some in Greek and others in Latin. He did this so that they would not have time to be occupied with gossip in church. He also composed and delivered very forceful sermons suited to the season and feast days.[26]

20. He had a very great concern for the sick and came to their assistance. He granted them a spacious house, in which they could listen undisturbed to the holy office [being sung] in the basilica. He set up beds and bedding, provided for expenses, and supplied a person to take care of them and heal them.[27] He did not deny to captives and the poor the place and opportunity to make requests. He regularly used to tell his attendant, "See whether any of the poor are standing at the doors, afraid and ashamed because of their poverty, lest for the sake of my own convenience and as a result of my own sinfulness they suffer any harm

---

[25] See for example his encyclical letter to bishops, preserved as *Serm.* 1.
[26] *Serm.* 187–232.
[27] For a history of such institutions in the Byzantine empire, see Miller (1985).

while waiting. [[For the responsibilities of our rank will not be properly fulfilled if we put off looking after and listening to the wretched, who are known to seek us out from different provinces because of their needs." When ransom had been given as the need arose, he released those who had been commended [to the church],[28] adding a prayer by which they might be protected.]][29] And drawing long sighs from the depths of his heart he used to say, "Truly Christ has become a babbler and talkative to the deaf; but nevertheless he asks, persuades, advises, and calls all to witness." He also used to say that the poor no doubt shared in our spiritual progress in the present world, because, with Christ as surety, we now commend to them on earth what we are later to receive in heaven.[30] [[Meanwhile, to obtain relief for the church of Arles the servant of God also went to see Alaric [II], king of the Visigoths, to whom at that time the city of Arles belonged. Caesarius was so reverently received by the king that although they were corrupted by the Arian heresy of barbarians, Alaric and his court nevertheless venerated the servant of Christ with great ceremony and respect, and enriched him as well. For Alaric furnished him with money that was to be used for the relief of captives. Moreover, through the assurance of a published edict he ordered that the church remain immune from taxation in perpetuity.]][31]

21. But a few days later, the envious adversity of the devil disturbed the tranquillity of this holy man, and since the devil could not accuse him of any carnal vices, he charged him with treason. Indeed, shortly afterwards a wicked man named Licinianus, one of his notaries, took on against this apostolic man the role that the apostle Judas had not feared to take on against our Savior. Equipped with the poison of a dire accusation, Licinianus asserted to king Alaric, through attendants,

[28] Captives were commended to the church to guarantee their redemption, Klingshirn (1985), 201, n. 135.
[29] This passage appears only in *codex Paris.*, B. N. lat. 5295. It is accepted by Krusch and Morin, but judged an interpolation by Cavallin (1934), 101.
[30] For example, in *Serm.* 25, 27, 29–31.
[31] This passage is also found only in *codex Paris.* B. N. lat 5295. Krusch accepts it; Cavallin condemns it; Morin is neutral. Cf. *Test.* 8, which states that Caesarius was awarded a tax immunity for church lands, but does not state its grantor. For other examples of the same privilege, see Lesne (1910–43) I, 258–60.

that since Caesarius had been born in [Burgundian] Gaul, he was trying with all his might to bring the territory and city of Arles under Burgundian rule.[32] He said this despite the fact that this most outstanding pastor regularly prayed to the Lord on bended knee day and night for the peace of the nations and the tranquillity of the cities—all the more reason to believe that it was at the devil's impulse that barbarian ferocity was stirred up to exile the holy man. For he who prays that the enemy's deeds might be opposed is not acceptable or pleasing to him. Therefore, at the urging of those present the king placed no faith in his innocence, and demanded no proof of the accusation. Instead, after being condemned by false and illegal allegations, Caesarius was taken from Arles and banished to the city of Bordeaux as if in exile [505].

22. But so that God's grace might not remain hidden in him, it happened one night that the city [of Bordeaux] was struck by a great fire. People quickly ran to the man of God and shouted, "By your prayers, holy Caesarius, extinguish the roaring flames!" When the man of God heard this, he was moved by sorrow and compassion. He prostrated himself in prayer in the face of the oncoming fire, and at once stopped the flames and drove them back. On seeing this, everyone praised God's manifestation of power in Caesarius. After this miracle everyone in Bordeaux admired him so much that they regarded him not only as a bishop but also as an apostle.[33] The devil, who had instigated his persecution, was thus thwarted when he saw that miracles of divine power brought renown to the man he had tried to accuse. We learned by a reliable report that the event happened this way.

23. And so he always instructed the church both there and everywhere "to render to God what belonged to God, and to Caesar what belonged to Caesar" [Matt. 22: 21], and further, in accordance with the

---

[32] Licinianus's intention was to have Caesarius deposed by Alaric, who had already deposed bishop Volusianus of Tours on a charge of intriguing with the Franks and would soon depose his successor Verus on the same grounds, Gregory of Tours, *Hist*. X. 31. 8. His motive may have been resentment at Caesarius's rapid rise to power ahead of more well qualified and senior local candidates. See further Schäferdiek (1967), 32–42, and Klingshirn (1994), 93–4.

[33] For St. Martin, the very model of a Gallic miracle-worker, as an "apostolic man," see Sulpicius Severus, *Vita Martini* 7.

apostle, to obey kings and magistrates when they give just orders [cf. Titus 3: 1], but to despise in a ruler the depravity of Arian teaching. When the truth was proclaimed in this fashion, the lamp placed upon a mountain could not be hidden, but wherever it went it enlightened all men as it shone atop the candelabrum of the Lord [cf. Matt. 5: 14–16].

24. After this, when he had ascertained the blessed man's innocence, the impious king ordered the holy bishop to return to his own church and present himself to the city and clergy. His accuser, however, the king ordered to be stoned.[34] And when people were assembling with stones in hand, the king's order suddenly reached Caesarius. The holy man quickly rose to intercede, for he did not want his accuser to be handed over for revenge. He asked instead through a personal request that the man be spared for penance, so that the Lord might cure through penance the soul that the devil had captured through the man's unwarranted betrayal. So by mercifully pardoning an adversary who belonged to his own household Caesarius could by his pure conscience conquer the ancient enemy twice in a single case.

25. The servant of God was particularly eager to observe the following rule, that no sinner, whether one of his slaves or the freeborn men under his control, should ever receive more than the legal number of lashes, that is thirty-nine.[35] But if someone was caught in a serious crime, Caesarius permitted him to be beaten again after several days with a few [more blows]. He warned the overseers of the church that if anyone ordered an offender to be beaten more than this and the man died from the punishment, the official responsible would be accused of murder.

26. When it was reported that the man of Christ was returning and was rapidly approaching the city [of Arles], the whole Christian

---

[34] This was the biblical punishment for betrayal and false witness, not the Roman or Visigothic punishment, Arnold (1894), 221. It is therefore more likely that if there was a decision to stone Licinianus, it was made by a Christian mob and not the king.

[35] This was a biblical prescription: Deut. 25: 3; 2 Cor. 11: 24.

community went out to meet him.[36] There, men and women holding tapers and crosses and singing psalms awaited the entrance of the holy man. Because Christ makes his people dance [with joy] at his wonderful deeds and confounds traitors by the clear light of his miracles, at the arrival of his servant the Lord covered the drought-stricken land with an abundant rain, so that the crops would flourish when the steward who was pleasing to him returned.

27. One day, as he looked down from the altar after the reading of the gospel, Caesarius saw some people leaving the church who particularly refused to listen to the word, that is the sermon, of the blessed man. Immediately he ran down and cried out to the people: "What are you doing, my children? Why are you being led outside? Have wicked thoughts overcome you? Stay here for a word of advice on behalf of your souls, and listen carefully! You will not be allowed to do this on Judgment Day![37] I warn you and call out to you. Do not desert or refuse to listen. Behold I affirm by the trumpet call of my voice that if anyone's soul is killed by the devil's sword, I shall not be declared guilty of keeping silent." Because of this he very often had the doors shut after the reading of the gospel until those who had once been deserters rejoiced by God's will at their chastisement and spiritual progress.

28. The man of God formulated the idea by divine inspiration from the ever-reigning Lord that the church of Arles should be adorned and the city protected not only with countless troops of clergy but also by choirs of virgins. In this way, while he remained alive, he might store up a full harvest in the heavenly granaries [like] a successful farmer, and after he had been received [into heaven], he might teach how this harvest was to be brought in by his followers.[38] But for some time the devil's envy stood in the way of these plans. For after king Alaric had been killed in battle by the most victorious king Clovis, and

[36] Commonly depicted in panegyrics and saints' lives, such scenes of imperial or episcopal arrival (*adventus*) represented the ceremonial expression of consensus, MacCormack (1981), 18.
[37] A similar episode occurs in the late fifth-century life of Caesarius's predecessor Hilarius, *Vita Hilarii* 18.
[38] For Caesarius's own use of this image, see *Serm.* 1. 10.

while the Franks and Burgundians were besieging the city, Theoderic, king of Italy, sent his generals ahead and entered Provence.[39] During this siege the monastery that Caesarius was beginning to have built for his sister and the other virgins was almost completely destroyed; its beams and upper rooms were ripped apart and overturned by savage barbarians.[40] And when he saw in ruins the work that he had been hastening to complete and had erected with his own hands and sweat, he was consumed by a double sorrow.

29. Then, utterly terrified by fear of captivity, a cleric who was also a fellow-citizen[41] and a relative of Caesarius was driven on by the capriciousness of youth and provoked by the inspiration of the devil against the servant of God. During the night he lowered himself over the wall by a rope. The next day the wicked traitor presented himself to the enemies besieging the city. When the Goths within the city learned of this, they attacked the holy man. A mob of people, including a crowd of Jews, shouted without restraint and charged that the bishop had sent his compatriot by night to betray the city to the enemy. No consideration was given to loyalty, proof, or a clear conscience. The heretics and especially the Jews leveled this charge without reverence or moderation. The bishop was taken from his official residence and placed under a tight guard in the palace.[42] The intention was either to drown him at night in the depths of the Rhône, or [failing that] to keep him prisoner in Beaucaire, so that[43] by his exile and his afflictions their hatred could rage on all the longer.

---

[39] Alaric was killed in the summer of 507 at the battle of Vouillé at which the Franks under Clovis defeated the Visigoths, Gregory of Tours, *Hist.* II. 37. Arles was besieged by a detachment of Franks and Burgundians later that year, and rescued in the autumn of 508 by the Ostrogoths. On Theoderic in Provence, see Procopius, *De bellis* V. 12. 44. On the causes and consequences of the battle, see Wood (1985); Wolfram (1988), 192–3; James (1988), 86–7; and Moorhead (1992), 178-83.

[40] Benoit (1935), 53, suggested that this monastery was located on the site of the medieval chapel of Saint-Césaire-le-Vieux.

[41] *Concivis*, probably a fellow-citizen of Chalon, as Aeonius also was (*Life* I. 10).

[42] Formerly the imperial palace in Arles.

[43] On this sense of *donec*, see *TLL* V. 1, col. 2003, lines 42–4.

30. The bishop's residence, including his bedchamber, was crowded with encampments of Arians. One of the Goths was reclining in the bishop's bed, although others told him not to do so. He was struck down by divine power and subsequently died.[44] The result was that none of the rest dared to violate the cell of God's servant with their filthy consciences. And when the Goths, because of God's will and the enemy siege, were unable to drive away[45] from either shore the cutter on which they had placed Caesarius, they brought the holy man back to the palace under cover of night and shrouded his whereabouts in silence, so that none of the catholics could know whether he was still alive.

31. This turn of events pleased the devil and delighted the Jews, who were spewing forth shameful charges against our people everywhere without any regard for their own treachery. One night, one of the Jewish troops stationed along the part of the city wall that the Jews happened to be responsible for guarding tied a letter to a stone and threw it at the enemy, pretending to strike them. In the letter he indicated his name and his religion and invited them to set their scaling ladders at night at the place the Jews guarded, provided that in return for the favor he offered, no Jew in the city should suffer captivity or plundering. But in the morning, when the enemy had retreated a little way from the wall, some of the citizens went outside the protecting wall among the rubble, as they were accustomed to do. On finding the letter they brought it back inside, and revealed its contents to everyone in the forum. Soon the traitor was brought forth, convicted, and punished. Then indeed the cruelty of the Jews that was savage to God and hateful to men was finally and openly destroyed.[46] Soon too our Daniel, that is holy Caesarius, was led out of the lion's den, and the accusation of the satraps was disproved [cf. Dan. 6: 23]. And a prophecy was fulfilled concerning the instigator of these events: "He opened up a pit and dug it out, and he fell into the ditch that he had made" [Ps. 7: 15].

[44] Saints' beds were thought to possess divine power, Van Dam (1985), 192.
[45] For *subrigere* as "drive away," see Cavallin (1934), 105–6.
[46] The circumstances in which this letter was composed and later found are transparently suspicious, as several commentators have noted. Juster

32. The Goths then returned to Arles with an immense number of captives. The sacred churches were filled with a crowd of unbelievers, as was even the bishop's residence. To those in great need the man of God gave sufficient food and clothing, until he could free them individually with the gift of redemption.[47] He first spent all the silver that his predecessor, the venerable Aeonius, had left for the bishop's table,[48] maintaining that the Lord had dipped bread into an earthen dish and not a silver cup [cf. Matt. 26: 23] and had advised his disciples not to possess gold or silver [cf. Matt. 10: 9]. His sacred work then proceeded all the way to the disposal of the church plate. And when the censers, chalices, and patens had been handed over for the redemption of these men, the consecrated ornaments of the church were sold for the redemption of the true church. Even today the blows of axes are visible on podiums and railings from which the silver ornaments of the small columns were cut away. For the man of God said that no rational man who had been redeemed by the blood of Christ should, as punishment for having lost his freedom, become perhaps an Arian or a Jew, or a slave instead of a free man or a slave of a man rather than of God.

33. Caesarius embellished and protected the church by this action; he did not disfigure it. He made the mother's womb open up with children; he did not cause it to be harmed.[49] Very often he said: "I would like to hear an explanation from any of my lord bishops or other clerics who because of greed do not wish to give the slaves of Christ inanimate silver or gold from the offerings of Christ. I repeat, I would like them to tell me, if such adversities happened to befall them, whether they would want to be freed by these inanimate offerings, or whether they would consider it a sacrilege if someone assisted them with these small

---

(1914) II, 213, suggests that the letter was forged by one of Caesarius's supporters. See also Lévi (1895) and Klingshirn (1994), 108–110.

[47] See further Klingshirn (1985).

[48] On this translation of *mensa ecclesiae* see *TLL* VIII, col. 740, line 5, rather than col. 742, lines 56–7, where the passage is cited. Aeonius had left this silver for the use of the bishop and those who dined with him, not for the poor; otherwise Caesarius would not have had to justify his actions.

[49] This symbolic language seems to refer to conversion, Klingshirn (1985), 199–202. For the "mother" as a symbol of the church, see Plumpe (1943). For the "womb" as a symbol of the baptismal font, see Bedard (1951), 17–36.

gifts dedicated to God. I do not believe it is contrary to God's wishes that ransom money be paid out from [the resources of] Christ's ministry, who gave himself for the redemption of mankind." From this we see that some praised the holy man's action, yet in no way emulated it. Was it not for us that the blood of Christ glistened in a glass chalice and his most precious body hung on the cross?

34. We, however, believe and trust in the Lord that it was through the compassion, faith, and prayers of the blessed Caesarius that although the city of Arles was besieged in his time, it did not deserve to suffer captivity or pillage. In this way then the city passed from the Visigoths to the kingdom of the Ostrogoths.[50] In the same way in the name of Christ it belongs today to the realm of the most glorious king Childebert,[51] for as we read, "They went from nation to nation, from a kingdom to another people, and God did not permit" anyone "to harm" his people of Arles under that ruler [Ps. 105: 13–14].

35. Meanwhile, Caesarius [rebuilt] in particular the monastery that he had begun to prepare for his sister, according to its original rule and with a cloister for [the protection of] virginity [512].[52] Since there is no obstacle to whatever befits the Christian mystery, like a latter-day Noah of our own time he fashioned an ark on account of storms and tempests. He built it for the companions and sisters on the side of the church.[53] He recalled from a monastery in Marseille[54] his venerable

---

[50] Following their defeat of Odovacar in 493, the Ostrogoths under king Theoderic had gained control over Italy. They remained in power under Theoderic's successors until 552 when king Teja was defeated by a Byzantine army at the battle of Milk Mountain. On Theoderic and the Ostrogoths in Italy see Wolfram (1988), 247–362, and Moorhead (1992).

[51] Childebert, son of Clovis, ruled Arles from 536/7 to his death in 558.

[52] The passage is corrupt, Cavallin (1934), 111–13. I take *singularitate* (= *singularitati*) as a dative of purpose, with the meaning "aloneness, chastity, virginity." On this sense, see de Vogüé–Courreau, 38.

[53] This church was located in the city's southeast corner, just within the walls. Originally the city's cathedral church, it probably lost that designation in the fifth century with the construction of a new cathedral church dedicated to St. Stephen and located near the forum, on the site of the present-day church of Saint-Trophime. For this view, see Benoit (1951) and Février (1986a), 80. For the view that the the city's original cathedral was still its

sister Caesaria whom he had sent there to learn what she would teach, and to be a pupil before becoming a teacher. He then set her up with two or three companions in the dwellings that he had prepared. Great numbers of virgins arrived there in throngs. By renouncing their property and parents they spurned the frail and deceptive blossoms of mortal existence and sought the lap of Caesarius, their father, and Caesaria, their mother. They did this so that—torches aflame—they might await with him entry into the kingdom of heaven,[55] and having entered properly might deserve to cling to the perpetual embraces of Christ. They are so strictly cloistered that until they die, none of the women are permitted to go outside the doors of the monastery.

36. For this reason, no doubt, and because of this devotion, the devil swelled up with anger like a raging lion at the servant of Christ. He again had the bishop taken from Arles on trumped-up charges, and led into Italy under guard all the way to Ravenna [513], so that the prophecy could be fulfilled in him: "Just as gold and silver are tested in a furnace, so the hearts of the chosen are tested in God's presence" [Prov. 17: 3]. He entered the palace and under the guidance of Christ approached king Theoderic to greet him. When the king saw the fearless and venerable man of God, he reverently stood up to greet him. When he had removed the royal insignia from his head, he greeted him again very cordially. First he questioned him about the difficulties of his journey and then affectionately inquired about his Goths and the people of Arles. After the holy bishop had gone out of his sight, the king addressed his courtiers: "Let God not spare those who have without just cause subjected this innocent and holy man to so long a journey. I recognized what sort of man he was by the fact that when he came in to greet me, I trembled all over. I see," he said, "the face of an angel. I see an apostolic man. I think it wrong to suppose any evil of so venerable a man."

37. Afterwards, when Caesarius had taken a room at an inn, the king sent him a silver dish as a gift for use at his table. It weighed

cathedral in Caesarius's day, having simply been re-dedicated to St. Stephen in the fifth century, see Hubert (1947) and de Vogüé–Courreau, 98–106.
[54] Probably Cassian's monastery for women.
[55] A paraphrase of Caesarius, *Regula virginum* 1.

about 60 pounds[56] and contained 300 additional *solidi*.[57] [With the
gift] he made a request: "Take this, holy bishop. Your son, the king,
asks that your blessedness worthily accept this vessel as a gift, and use
it in his memory." But Caesarius, who never used any silver at his
table except spoons,[58] had the dish appraised by his attendants and on
the third day sold in public. With its proceeds he started to free many
captives. Soon, they say,[59] the king's retainers announced to him,
"Behold, we saw your lord's gift put up for sale in the marketplace.
With its price the holy Caesarius is ransoming crowds of captives.
Indeed, so many poor people were crowded into his lodgings, and the
entrance hall of his house was so congested, that it was hardly possible
to approach him to say hello because of the sheer number of poor men
making their requests to him. We also saw countless groups of unfortunate people running about the streets and going to him repeatedly."

38. When he learned of this action, Theoderic admired and praised
it so much that all the senators and leading men in attendance at his
palace competed in wishing for the blessed man to distribute the price
of their gifts with his right hand. For they proclaimed that they had
been blessed by God, because they were worthy of beholding such a
bishop, who appeared in those times apostolic by his words and deeds, a
true successor of the apostles. And because nothing flies swifter than
fame, his very holy work was widely publicized, and the holy reputation of the blessed man soon traveled to Rome. There, the senate, the
leading men, the Pope, the clergy, and the people began to yearn so fer-
vently [for his arrival] that before he was seen in person he won the affection of people's hearts. Meanwhile, in Italy he soon discovered and
ransomed all the captives he could from beyond the Durance, especially
from Orange.[60] This city had been completely enslaved, and he had al-

[56] At about 330 grams the Roman pound was lighter than the English
pound.
[57] The *solidus* was a gold coin weighing $1/72$ of a Roman pound.
[58] Like Augustine, Possidius, *Vita Augustini* 22.
[59] This verb indicates that the bishops' narrative was based on the eyewitness report of others, possibly the notary Messianus and others who traveled with him, *Life* I. 40.
[60] Orange was located in territory north of the river Durance that was
claimed by the metropolitan bishops of Arles and Vienne alike. By ransoming natives of the region, Caesarius demonstrated his charitable zeal and as-

ready redeemed part of its inhabitants in Arles. Moreover, to make their liberty more complete, he sent them on their way with provisions, horses, and wagons, and with the assistance and organization of his own officials he arranged for their return home.

39. There was at this time in the aforementioned city of Ravenna a widow whose young son served in the office of the prefect and supported his poor mother with the fees he received and his salary.[61] The young man had been stricken with a sudden illness and was lying unconscious. When there was no more hope of a human cure and no more consolation for him, his mother left him behind and ran in haste to the man of God. Her body prostrate and her eyes moist with tears, she wailed in lamentation. Emboldened only by the strength of her faith, she embraced the knees of the blessed man and called out, "I believe that divine mercy has led you here, holy one of God, so that you might return a son to his mother." At first, he declined to help the woman who tearfully begged for his help. Nevertheless, believing himself hard-hearted if he did not heed such tears, he was moved by his customary compassion. Yet he wanted to carry out the charitable duty that he felt and work a miracle in God's name in such a way that he avoided vanity in all things. And so he went to her cottage secretly.

40. He prayed, prostrate in his usual fashion, and departed when he perceived that divine power had come through the Holy Spirit at his invocation. He left behind Messianus, who served as his notary at the time, but who is now a venerable priest, and instructed him to report to him as soon as the young man regained consciousness. While Messianus kept watch at the patient's bedside, after not even an hour had gone by, the young man was called back from the shadows of death. Soon he opened his eyes and addressed his mother: "Mother, go and hurry to the servant of God, by whose prayers I was returned to you and to life, and thank him, because God granted success to his merits and virtues." She swiftly ran to Caesarius and thanked him not so much in words as in tears, cries, and expressions of joy. She further requested

---

serted his claim to metropolitan control at the same time. See further Klingshirn (1985), 194.

[61] For the duties, grades, and incomes of civil servants in the office of the praetorian prefect, see Jones (1964) I, 586–92.

that her son whom God had returned to this light through Caesarius not be permitted to depart from his service when he returned to Gaul. But blessed Caesarius, a man of profound wisdom, replied that she ought to give thanks rather to him whose virtue and piety came to all who deserved them and to all who mourned. Because of the prayers and reports of the faithful, news of this great miracle traveled not only through that city, but also through the whole province.

41. The deacon Helpidius, who was also a physician and was very close to the king and zealously served him, suffered from a demonic infestation.[62] He was not only worn out by various other afflictions, but was also frequently assaulted by showers of stones in his own house. He convinced the holy man of God that he deserved to be freed from this distress by his prayers. Upon entering his house to purify it, Caesarius sprinkled it with holy water and so thoroughly delivered it from the perils of its previous distress that nothing similar has ever happened there since.

42. After this he arrived in Rome and was introduced to blessed Symmachus, the pope at that time, and then to the senators and their wives.[63] Everyone thanked God and king Theoderic because they had been thought worthy of seeing with their corporeal eyes the man whom they had for so long observed with the eyes of their heart. And while approving of the apostolic man no longer on the basis of his reputation but on the basis of his actual presence, they began to vie with one another in esteeming and venerating him. For this reason pope Symmachus too, being moved by the great worthiness of Caesarius's good deeds and by a great reverence for his sanctity, not only most properly honored him as metropolitan, but also decorated him by the

---

[62] Helpidius, whose medical skill was highly regarded throughout Gaul and Italy (Avitus of Vienne, *Epist.* 38), served as Theoderic's court physician. That he also became a confidant of the king is revealed by Procopius's report that shortly before his death Theoderic confessed to Helpidius his remorse for having executed the philosopher Boethius, *De bellis* V. 1. 38. See further *PLRE* II, 537 (Helpidius 6).

[63] Symmachus was bishop of Rome from 498 to 514. See the introduction to *Letter* 6 for details of his career.

specially granted privilege of the *pallium*.[64]   He also distinguished
Caesarius's deacons by allowing them to wear dalmatics in the fashion
of Roman deacons.[65]

43. From there he returned home.   Upon entering the city of
Arles, he was welcomed with the singing of psalms.   Having left to be
exiled, he brought back with him from Italy 8000 *solidi*, [even] after
paying out the ransom money.   Indeed, on the day he came into the
city, he entered the church to give the blessing at Vespers.   And—mark
this!—a woman who was trembling and foaming at the mouth burst
into the church.   Her wailing and shouting terrified the whole congregation.   Some of the bystanders grabbed her and immediately brought her
to the blessed man before the altar.   Everyone prevailed upon him to
drive out the affliction and restore the woman to health.   Then, in his
usual way, he stretched himself forth in prayer before her.   Putting his
hand on her head, he anointed her eyes, ears, nose, mouth, and face with
a dab of sacred oil.   When he had done this, the illness was driven out
in the name of Christ and it never again troubled the woman.

44. In the meantime, among other concerns he had a special concern for captives, and he was so outstanding and famous in this form of
assistance that no one can possibly tell the whole story.   For example,
one day when his holy hands lacked gold or silver coins to give the
needy, he said to a beggar who had accosted him, "What can I do for
you, my poor man?   I will give you what I have."   And entering his
cell he brought out a white paschal processional cloak that he owned
and gave it to him.   He said, "Go and sell this to a cleric, and ransom
your captive from its price."   For not only were those who sought him
out freed from the bonds of captivity, but he also proceeded to
Carcassonne on his own to ransom captives.[66]   And also in many

---

[64] The *pallium* was a band of wool decorated with crosses and worn over the
shoulders by the bishop of Rome and other bishops to whom he had given
his permission.   For details, see Braun (1907), 620–76.

[65] The dalmatic was a white tunic made of linen or wool with two red stripes
reaching over the shoulders from front to back.   Further details in Braun
(1907), 249–302.

[66] Carcassonne was located not in Caesarius's ecclesiastical province but in
the province of Narbonensis I, which was administered by the metropolitan
bishop of Narbonne.   By extending his patronage to captives in the city

villages throughout various regions he sent abbots, deacons, and clerics to ransom the unfortunate.

45. By himself he was worthy to possess more gifts of divine grace than many of the servants of God have had together. Yet he always cultivated each one of these gifts in himself as if it were the only one he had. His most endearing and pleasant qualities seemed to surpass all others until they were surpassed by those that followed. For who could describe his patience, his purity, his charity, his passion for [things of] the Spirit, his discretion, his kindliness, his holy zeal, his constant meditation day and night on the Lord's law? [Even] when he seemed to stop meditating on the psalms or preaching, a lector or a notary did not cease reading to him. He was a defender of the faith, pattern for bishops, ornament of the churches, preacher of grace, extinguisher of quarrels, seed-garden of charity, standard of instruction, assessor of character, balance of counsel, defense of orphans, and ransom of captives. Never did he utter a slander, a lie, or a curse against anyone. And not only did he never disparage anyone, but he did not tolerate anyone who disparaged someone else. If any one of his subordinates suddenly swore an oath or perhaps uttered a curse, then depending on who the person was, he punished him appropriately for his own good. If he was ever moved to anger against anyone, this was the blessing he used in place of a curse: "May God wipe out your sin; may God take away your sins; may the Lord reprove your fault. May God reprove your error here so that it does not remain with you there."

46. His appearance revealed his inner self. For he was always of a placid and angelic countenance, and in the words of scripture, his face shone because of his joyful heart [cf. Prov. 15: 13]. Just as he was never too relaxed when laughing at the appropriate time, so he was never depressed by excessive sadness, except perhaps when he was mourning for the sins of others. He never hated anyone, and he prayed with heartfelt affection not only for friends but also for enemies. He did not teach in words what he did not fulfill by example. No hour of the

Caesarius probably did not intend to claim the province as his own. Rather, he seems to have been acting to ransom natives of his own province on behalf of the bishop of Narbonne, whose city had been pillaged by Burgundian warriors in 507/8 and was in no position to help others.

day passed him by without meditation on the divine word, not even
when he was sleeping; indeed, he frequently seemed to sleep and medi-
tate at the same time, so that he might rightly and truly say, "The meditation of my heart is always in your sight" [Ps. 19: 14].

47. Once when he traveled around the Alpilles[67] with the venerable and holy bishop Eucherius,[68] they happened to meet a poor sick
woman in the middle of the road. Because her hands and feet were crippled, she was crawling along the ground. When he noticed her, he
asked holy Eucherius why she was dragging herself over the ground this
way. He then questioned the woman. She responded that she had been
paralyzed for many years and that all her limbs were crippled. Then
blessed Caesarius said to the holy Eucherius, "Dismount and make the
sign of the cross over her." He began to get agitated and make excuses.
But Caesarius said he would not stop urging him until he did it. So
Eucherius dismounted, blessed her, and said, "There. I have done what
you ordered." Caesarius responded, "Now extend your hand, take her
hand, and lift her up." He answered, "I shall do whatever else you order
me to do, but I shall not presume to do this. Do it yourself, for God
has given you the power to cure both the souls and the bodies of the afflicted." Caesarius answered, "Nevertheless, do what I tell you." And
when Eucherius boldly resisted and humbly and tearfully made excuses
and persisted in this for a long time, Caesarius asked him, "How were
you going to enter fire out of obedience when you were not even prepared to do out of mercy what love commands? Extend your hand in
the name of the Lord, and raise her up." Then, obeying his orders,
Eucherius extended his hand and lifted the woman up. And with her feet
and arms healed she walked back home unimpaired.

48. Who could fully explain the many miracles for which he was
known? It happened that in a suburban field of his monastery wild
boars used to gather. The counts of the city and the rest of the soldiers
used to go out and did not permit the peasants of that household to

---

[67] A chain of mountains in the northern part of the diocese.
[68] Eucherius was a bishop in Caesarius's province who attended the councils
of Arles (524), Carpentras (527), Orange (529), and Marseille (533). His
see is unknown. He may be identical with the Eucherius 5 in Heinzelmann
(1982), 598–9.

work; instead they beat them viciously because they kept the boars away. Finally, no longer willing to tolerate these injuries and disturbances, they came and beseeched their master [Caesarius]. "Do what you want with us," they exclaimed, "for we can neither serve you nor stay there." Caesarius solicitously asked what their complaints were. They answered, "Because of the wild boars, counts, Goths and other hunters come and maltreat us." Then he raised his eyes and hands, looked into heaven, and said in a loud voice, "Lord Jesus Christ, do not ever again permit boars to enter that field." From that very hour until the present the boars have never fed there as they had been accustomed to do, nor has there ever appeared there any prey that could be hunted. Having driven all vice from himself, he was entitled to command the beasts. He could request this from God, whose Law he had never transgressed.

49. It also happened that a slave of the illustrious patrician Parthenius[69] whom his master considered outstanding and preferred to his other slaves often fell down unconscious on the ground as the result of a wicked attack. And since the attack by his enemy seemed in fact to be a spiritual affliction rather than a physical infirmity, he was anointed with holy oil that had been consecrated by the blessed man. After this, the evil affliction departed from him so completely that his master even put him in charge of his household. Through his servant Christ had restored him to good health after the treatment of a physician of this world had failed.

50. As an example of terror that can arouse more admiration than fear, it is wrong to pass over in silence this memorable deed of his that demonstrates the merit of the holy man. While Caesarius was making the rounds of his parishes, he was welcomed at the villa of Launico by its owners.[70] After his departure, in the room in which he had slept and

[69] Parthenius was the grandson of Ruricius of Limoges and nephew of Ennodius, Mathisen (1981), 101–2; Heinzelmann (1982), 663. His wife's grandfather was the emperor Avitus (455–6). He held several posts in Gaul under the Ostrogoths and Franks, *PLRE* II, 833–4 (Parthenius 3). Some years after having his wife murdered on suspicion of adultery, he was himself killed by a mob angry with his oppressive taxation, Gregory of Tours, *Hist.* III. 36.
[70] The location of this villa is unknown.

on the covers [of his bed], a dissolute physician named Anatolius sought out the services of a prostitute. He was to be very sorry for such a sin, for he was soon seized with trembling in public by the devil that had incited him. In the sight of everyone he was knocked to the ground, and in the process of acknowledging the power of the servant of God, he publicly confessed the audacious crime for which he had been seized.

51. Indeed, we know that the Lord has performed many miracles through the intercession of the man of God, which it would take too long to relate one by one. For example, one of the authors of this text had requested for his own use some consecrated oil that Caesarius had blessed. He tried to protect the full bottle that he received from him, and carefully carried it home as the most precious of relics. And when after some time he was oppressed by the terrible burning of a tertian fever, he asked that the vessel containing the oil be suspended over his head with great reverence as a powerful protection. When the bottle had been wrapped up in the purest linen cloth, it was broken—by the negligence of the slaves, we think. But the bottle retained its oil so completely that no liquid dripped onto the ground or into the cloth. When this was observed, the oil was very quickly transferred into another container. Once it had been completely emptied, the broken bottle immediately fell apart. With the help of the Lord the fever immediately departed from the man who accurately recalls these things.

52. Who could describe how skilfully he discussed the scriptures and elucidated obscure verses? His ability was such that he received the greatest pleasure out of being invited by someone to explain difficult passages. And he very frequently used to encourage us by saying, "I know that you do not know everything. Why do you not ask, so that you can learn? For cows do not always run to calves, but sometimes calves hurry toward the cows, so that they might be able to satisfy their hunger from their mothers' udders. You should certainly do this also so that by asking questions, you might keep us occupied with our duty to find a source of spiritual honey for you." Woe to me, wretched Cyprianus! I have been so indifferent to learning that only now do I understand and repent! Why did I not draw as much from this great flowing fountain as my parched soul required?

53. All the individual virtues shone out in him, namely, virginity with sincerity, modesty with shame, wisdom with simplicity, severity with mildness, teaching with humility, in short, an unstained life, an irreproachable life, and a life always equal to the man himself. Who could ever imitate the fervor of the charity with which he loved all men? For he used to convey this virtue especially in his heart and on his lips, and he used laudably to instruct us by the most agreeable exhortation, by speech, and by example that we ought to love our enemies. Hardly anyone prays for his dearest loved ones with as much affection as he used to pray for his enemies. And although there was no reason why anyone would be his enemy (except perhaps those who seemed to be his rivals because of hatred or because of his teachings), he nevertheless used to esteem these with not only a paternal but also a maternal affection. He often pointed out to us that when we love even our enemies, we can never fail to love our neighbor as well.

54. He taught from memory[71] as often as he could, and always preached in a loud voice in church. He was so piously and energetically concerned for this duty that when sickness prevented him from carrying it out, he appointed and instructed priests and deacons to fulfill this task by preaching in church.[72] He did this so that no bishop might easily excuse himself on any grounds from providing this exhortation, which was necessary to everyone. For he said, "If priests and deacons read the words of the Lord, the prophets, and the apostles, why should they not read the words of Ambrose, Augustine, my humble self, or any of the holy [fathers]?[73] 'No slave is greater than his master' [John 15: 20]. I believe that those who have been given the authority to read the gospel are also permitted to recite in church the sermons of the servants of God or their explanations of the canonical scriptures. I absolve myself by establishing this practice. Holy bishops who disdain to do this should realize that they will plead their cases on Judgment Day. I do not be-

---

[71] *Memoriter* here probably refers not to verbatim memory, but to that "memory for things" recommended to orators by the rules of classical rhetoric. See further Klingshirn (1994), 12–14.

[72] This practice was instituted for the province of Arles by the Council of Vaison (529), can. 2, *CCSL* 148A (1963), 78-9. For its background see Beck (1950), 267–9.

[73] A paraphrase of *Serm.* 1. 15.

lieve that anyone to whom God says, 'Cry out, do not desist' [Isa. 58: 1] would be so hard-hearted that he would neither cry out himself nor permit others to do so. He should fear this verse: 'Woe to those who are quiet about you, for the talkative ones are mute' [cf. Isa. 6: 5], and this verse from the apostle [*sic*]: 'mute dogs, unable to bark' [Isa. 56: 10]. Indeed, if a bishop is silent, he will have to account for the souls of as many of his flock as have wandered away."

55. He delivered sermons suited to particular feasts and scriptural passages,[74] and also against the evil of drunkenness and lust, against discord and hatred, against anger and pride, against the sacrilegious and fortune-tellers, against the utterly pagan rites of the Kalends [of January],[75] and against augurs, worshippers of trees and springs, and vices of different kinds.[76] He prepared these sermons in such a way that if any visitor requested them, he did not refuse to share them.[77] Even if his visitor did not suggest that he ought to take any of them, Caesarius nonetheless offered them to him to read and brought them to him. To clerics located far away in the Frankish lands, Gaul, Italy, Spain, and other provinces, he sent through their bishops sermons they could preach in their own churches, so that when they had cast aside frivolous and perishable things, they might become, according to the apostle, "followers of good deeds" [Titus 2: 14]. In this way he diffused the fragrance of Christ far and wide. Through his accomplishments he burned

[74] The phrase *praedicationes ... congruas ... locis* would normally mean "sermons suitable to places," as Hillgarth (1986) has translated it, 41. But in this context *loci* may be better taken to mean scriptural passages, since as note 76 *infra* explains, the sentence would then constitute a comprehensive description of Caesarius's surviving sermons.
[75] *Serm.* 192, 193. This celebration is studied in Meslin (1970) and Arbesmann (1979).
[76] This sentence constitutes a comprehensive description of the surviving corpus of Caesarius's sermons. As Morin has organized them, *Serm.* 187–232 are devoted to feasts (including martyrs' feasts), *Serm.* 81–186 are dedicated to biblical exegesis, and *Serm.* 1–80 and 233–238 attack drunkenness, anger, and other vices and pagan practices.
[77] The surviving introduction to one of these collections (*Serm.* 2) further specifies that because the copyists in Arles were still inexperienced, the recipient should emend the text where necessary and have the sermons recopied in a better hand and on parchment before sending the collection on to other parishes.

brightly, [even] where he himself never appeared. He touched the hearts of those he never met in person.

56. He also decreed that he would never ordain a deacon in his church before the age of thirty.[78] He also added the provision that no one any older would be ordained unless he had read the books of the Old and New Testaments four times in order. Sinner that I am, I affirm to your holy conscience that whatever he ordered others to do or did himself, he always completed everything for God. Whether forbidding an action or avoiding one himself, everything he did or felt reflected his zeal for God; nothing was unspiritual.

57. And because he never wanted to rest from God's work, he designed and built a triple basilica in a single enclosure [524].[79] He built the nave in honor of the holy Virgin Mary and adorned it more prominently. Of the side aisles, one was devoted to St. John, the other to St. Martin. To relieve the holy virgins he had gathered [in his monastery] of concern for the demands of burial, he had monolithic sarcophagi suitable for burying the dead freshly cut out of huge stones. He then had these arranged in dense rows over the floor of the whole basilica, so that any of the sisters who passed from this life might find a holy burial place ready for use.

---

[78] This was five years higher than the minimum age set at Agde (506), can. 17, *CCSL* 148 (1963), 201, and Arles (524), can. 1, *CCSL* 148A (1963), 43.

[79] This was most likely the same church of St. Mary that was dedicated at the council of Arles in 524. The question of its location is closely tied to the location of the cathedral church at the time. Benoit (1951) and Février (1964), 67–9, have argued that the church of St. Mary was located on the site of the original cathedral church next to the monastery and within the city walls. In contrast, Hubert (1947) and de Vogüé–Courreau, 106–11, have argued that it was located outside the walls, in the belief that the original cathedral was still in use next to the monastery. At the moment, archaeological evidence seems to favor the view of Benoit and Février, but only a thorough excavation of the site can answer the question definitively.

58. Not long after this his sister, holy Caesaria [the Elder],
mother of the monastery, passed on to the rewards of Christ.[80] He
buried her among the sisters he had buried there before, between the altar and his episcopal throne,[81] next to the grave he had prepared for
himself. She was succeeded as mother [superior] by Caesaria [the
Younger], who is still alive. Her work with her companions is so outstanding that in the midst of psalms and fasts, vigils and readings, the
virgins of Christ beautifully copy out the holy books, with their
mother herself as teacher.

59. And so, as he was accustomed, the blessed man used to devote
himself unceasingly to prayer, reading, almsgiving, and—every Sunday
and feast day—to preaching. Often he also delivered homilies at Matins
and Vespers for the benefit of visitors, so that no one could claim ignorance as an excuse. He used to summon those who obeyed, instruct
those who were anxious, and sharply warn those who resisted him that
just as a suitable reward would necessarily be conferred on the faithful
on Judgment Day, so too would a fittingly wrathful punishment be
meted out to them. He also established the rule that newlyweds should
be blessed in church three days before the consummation of their marriage, out of reverence for the ritual of benediction.[82] In short, because
of the progress of his listeners, the obedience of his pupils, and the
consecration of virgins he had so many gifts bestowed on him by divine
grace that he has not been crowned for only one merit, but because of
his shimmering merits, he is now encircled by so many crowns that he
is completely transformed into a crown of glory.

[80] Caesaria the Elder died between 524, when the burial church was dedicated, and the council of Valence (528), the next datable event in the *Life* (I.
60).
[81] For this translation of *ad medium troni*, see Fixot (1986), 118.
[82] In imitation of Tobias and his wife (Tobit 6: 18, 22), married couples
were supposed to abstain from sexual relations for the first three days of
marriage, Payer (1980), 365. The *Statuta ecclesiae antiqua*, can. 101, *CCSL*
148 (1963), 184–5, advised a single night for the same reason.

60. And indeed many rivals arose who opposed his doctrine of grace.[83]   But what happiness it was to be hated [for this reason]! Indeed, because of the muttering of certain men and their wicked interpretations a sinister suspicion arose in parts of Gaul against the preaching of the man of God—albeit in vain.   On account of this the bishops of Christ located beyond the Isère met in the city of Valence, having been brought together by a love of charity.[84]   Blessed Caesarius could not attend the meeting as he had planned because of a serious illness. But he sent the most outstanding bishops [in his place], accompanied by priests and deacons, among whom holy Cyprianus, the distinguished bishop of Toulon, stood out prominently.   Cyprianus proved everything Caesarius had been saying from the divine scriptures, and demonstrated from the most ancient pronouncements of the fathers that no one could make any advance in divine progress on his own unless he had first been called by the intervention of God's grace.   But while they were seeking to establish their own justice, they did not observe God's justice.   They did not remember that God had said, "Without me you can do nothing" [John 15: 5] and "I have chosen you; you have not chosen me" [John 15: 16], and "no one has anything, unless it has been given him from above" [John 19: 11].   Nor did they remember that the apostle had said, "By the grace of God I am what I am" [1 Cor. 15: 10], and that another apostle had said, "Every good gift is from above" [Jas. 1: 17], and that a prophet had said, "The Lord will give grace and glory" [Ps. 84: 11].   And they did not remember that man truly recovers his free will when he has been redeemed by the liberation of Christ, and that as a result of this absolution he can take up the pursuit of perfection.   [Soon] the man of Christ provided a true and obvious solution to their disputes from apostolic tradition.[85]   At that point Boniface of blessed memory, bishop of Rome, became aware of this controversy and confirmed by apostolic authority the course of action by which holy Caesarius had settled the dispute among those who were

[83] Caesarius favored a moderate position on grace, against the extremes of predestination and Pelagianism alike.   For an overview of the dispute, see Vogt (1980), 722–8, and Markus (1989).
[84] The council of Valence was convened by bishop Julianus of Vienne, probably in 528.   Its canons do not survive.
[85] At the council of Orange (529).   For a translation of its canons, see Burns (1981), 109–28.

quarreling.[86] By Christ's gift the bishops of the churches gradually restored [the consensus] that the devil had hoped would cease because of their unexpected animosity.

61. Frequently he preached the following to people: "If you love the word of God you will certainly retain in your hearts what I have instilled in them. Indeed, the highest perfection of the Ten Commandments consists of divine love; so that what the love of Christ has won for itself in you, you should have in common with others by sharing your abundance. But do not assume that our sermon is only intended to nourish the souls of your relatives, friends, and tenants.[87] I solemnly declare in the presence of God and his holy angels that you will be held responsible for the salvation of any of your slaves who happen to be sick, if when you return you do not take back to them as well as to your friends and relatives what we have preached.[88] For you should know that a slave is subjected to you in the present by his earthly status, but is not enslaved by an eternal bond." And again he used to say to his audience, "What have we said, brothers? What have we discussed, my sons? I ask you, what have we said so far in the discussion? If you love, you remember; if you remember, you have undoubtedly taken up our words into your hearts." By challenging his audiences in this way he used to force even reluctant listeners to try to remember [what he said].

62. Every day at lunch and dinner there were readings without interruption at his table, so that both the interior and the exterior man might rejoice at being filled up with a double feast. I myself admit that his listeners broke into a sweat in these narrow quarters, and many to their great shame soon demonstrated their forgetfulness in front of him. Even worse, few could repeat in a quick summary the brief story read to them. Whether he was absent or present, a meal was always ready for clerics or other visitors in the bishop's quarters. While he was alive, no visitor came to Arles as if it were a strange city, but as if it were his own home. [[With great zeal and spiritual fervor he took care of churches, monasteries, pilgrims, widows, and the sick. He used to pray

---

[86] Caesarius, *Letter* 20, dated 25 January 531.
[87] For the translation of *clientes* as "tenants," see Bieler (1937).
[88] Caesarius makes similar suggestions in *Serm.* 13. 4; 33. 4; 193. 4.

on their behalf that no one be unjustly oppressed. He welcomed all his visitors with so charitable a disposition and spoke with such holy and sweet conversation that whoever came into his presence believed that he had acquired a share of eternal happiness. No women, however, were permitted to enter the bishop's house, whether to greet him or for any reason. This included nuns, female relatives, and slave girls. This was truly a holy, careful, and excellent custom, intended to remove every evil occasion and sinister suspicion.]][89]

63. Now that we have touched upon these few of his innumerable good deeds, let what we have revealed suffice, even if we have left some things unsaid. Now we ask you, the priest Messianus and the deacon Stephanus, our holy brothers, to attach your account here to our work, for you have learned much about him as a result of serving him from your youth.

[89] This passage is found in *codex Paris.*, B. N. lat. 5295 alone; Cavallin (1934) considered it an interpolation, 102–4.

THE LIFE OF CAESARIUS
BOOK II

Here ends the first book and begins the second.

1. Here is what the priest Messianus and the deacon Stephanus said. In discussing the way of life and miracles of lord Caesarius, our holy and most blessed father, bishop, and master, we are going to narrate what we know about him either in common or individually, and what we have seen together with his most holy fellow bishops, that is, lord Cyprianus, lord Firminus, and holy Viventius. Having started the previous narrative about Caesarius at the beginning and concluded it at the end of the section, they have deigned to allow and to order each of us to recount faithfully those actions of Caesarius that he knows well. We do not stand in need of secular eloquence, even if it were available to us, for the truth of holy actions transcends every ornament of worldly eloquence. To demonstrate this truth most fully, let the same purity and simplicity suffice for us as enabled our most blessed father to work the miracles we are going to recount. This is especially true since our master himself frequently said in his public sermons that what was said in a learned fashion would only educate the learned, but what was said in a simple fashion would suitably instruct the learned and simple alike.[90] And so, to the best of our ability, we shall begin, God willing, to make known to our faithful listeners in unvarnished and irreproachable language what we know he truly did or said, so that from his words and deeds compunction might be furnished to the sick, joy to the perfect, and a good example to those on the way to perfection. So with God's assistance we shall begin to briefly narrate his holy deeds just as we remember them.

2. Peter, a deacon of this church, had a daughter who was indispensable in managing his household. She lay mute for three days afflicted with a debilitating weakness. Peter therefore prostrated himself one day at the feet of the blessed man and said, "Servant of Christ, have mercy on my old age; come and pray for my daughter, for I believe that the Lord will deny you nothing. Put your hand over her and she will be well; already for three days she has been lying silent with her eyes

---

[90] Cf. *Serm.* 86. 1.

closed, and each hour and minute I expect her to die." Moved by these words and spurred on by the old man's tears, Caesarius went to his house. When he had entered and seen everyone in the house weeping profusely with the father, he prostrated himself in prayer. Then, like a second Elisha [cf. 2 Kgs. 4: 34], he drew himself up to her head in the narrow space between the chest and the bed. After a tearful prayer he immediately returned to his residence.

3. It was his custom to depart immediately as soon as he learned from the Holy Spirit that his prayers for the sick had been heard. This was to prevent any occasion for arrogance from arising if what he had asked the Lord in his prayers came to pass in his presence. Indeed he often used to say (agreeably, but more or less allusively, so that no one could understand), "The person entrusted with the care of the soul should greatly fear to take care of bodies. For divine grace has granted this ability to the simple rather than to the learned. May the merciful Lord grant us the caution that is pleasing to himself in using the power he has given us, unworthy as we are. We must not take this for granted."

4. Then, as the bishop was departing, the girl's father began to shout over and over after him, "I know that if you have called upon your Lord, my daughter will be returned to me." Then Caesarius left behind one of his chamber servants. "Go and keep watch there," he said, "and after a little while come and tell me what is happening." Not even an hour had passed when—behold!—he announced, "Lord, the girl over whom you prayed has regained consciousness. She said, 'The lord bishop was here, who restored me and made me well by his prayers.' For this reason her father has come giving thanks and has announced in public that his daughter has just been brought back to him from death through your prayers." Indeed, because the Lord granted this, she is to-day a living witness of this miracle.

5. But although it is always customary for the servants of God to refuse to perform miracles, this servant of Christ in particular, even when he was confident at the time, because the Lord suggested it, that an opportunity for him to perform a miracle was at hand, did not want to be overbold in seizing it, but tried carefully to avoid it. Yet, whether

he stayed or left, God was never absent when he called upon him. He had him in his heart not only in prayer and entreaty, but also at meals and on journeys, in conversation and in solitude,[91] and in prosperity and adversity; even in his sleep he always had him with him.[92] Indeed, we ourselves and our fellow servants who stayed in his cell know what we are talking about. Between the interruptions in his sleep that his age not only required but also sometimes demanded because of sickness— his spirit being ever vigilant—he used to say, "Come now, speak," as though he were advising someone to recite a psalm. No one doubts that he used to sing psalms spiritually with the saints or that he certainly fulfilled that saying of the prophet, "I sleep, and my heart remains on watch" [S. of S. 5: 2]. Frequently while asleep he used to preach about the future judgment and the eternal reward. Now, it is with no thanks to my own merits that I unworthily relate some remarkable stories about the servant of God.[93]

6. When by my own choice I had been assigned to his cell as a deacon in his service, he ordered me among other duties to take charge of the prayers of the night office.[94] Once [to determine the time] I had gone outside the inner part of the cell where I usually stayed.[95] Because the holy man always wanted to maintain moderation in all things, he used to watch most carefully, especially around the time of the night office, so that—except when someone wanted to pray by himself in God's presence alone—none of his clerics who used to stay with him should be awakened before the proper hour. On that occasion he kept

[91] For *consessu*, I read *concessu*, Norberg (1968), 101.
[92] This is a paraphrase of *Serm.* 1. 10 and 13. 4.
[93] The narrator is Stephanus.
[94] These prayers, which consisted of psalms, readings, and hymns (Caesarius, *Regula virginum* 68, 69), were held at varying hours of the night, depending on the season. Caesarius's rules for monks and nuns do not state the times explicitly. In *Regula Benedicti* 8. 1 night prayers were held at the eighth hour of the night, that is, around 2 or 3 a.m. See Table 4 in Biarne (1981), 113.
[95] The telling of time was essential for monastic prayer schedules, but in a world without mechanical clocks, it was difficult to determine the time at night. Observations of the stars and close attention to rooster calls were the main methods in use. See further, Biarne (1981), 115–17.

whispering in his sleep,[96] "There are two places, there is no middle place, only two: either one ascends into heaven or descends into hell."[97] When I returned to the cell from outside, he awoke and said to me, "What is it? Is it already time for the night office?" I answered, "It is not time yet; it is still early." And he replied, "It really is time." And so it was. Then after we completed the night prayers, he said to me, "I was strenuously crying out to someone in a dream, 'There are two places, two places, there is no middle place, either one goes into hell or heaven.'" I replied, "You make it your habit to call out unceasingly." At that moment, as a sinner myself, I thought he was always speaking about God and with him.

7. He was, as we said above, such a lover of all the virtues that there was no good deed that he did not either eagerly perform on his own or teach and desire others to perform with spiritual fervor. Among all the good actions, then, that he used to teach should always be done and all the wicked actions that he used to proclaim should never be done, he utterly abhorred in particular, as your kindly and sincere conscience knows, the vices of unbelief,[98] lying, pride, luxury, and (least tolerantly of all) drunkenness. Sweet Jesus, with what groans, with what sighs, with what weeping did he pray for sinners! So much so that you knew that the man of God was watching the wretched sinner being bound over for the punishments of hell, just as if [it were happening] at that very moment. Indeed, according to the precepts of the apostle, he never lived for himself alone [cf. Rom. 14: 7] and never prayed for himself alone.

8. On one occasion, as if to add to his merits, when captives from all over were being brought to Arles to be ransomed—with good reason—a great multitude of those who had already been released, including free-born people and many nobles, were being fed daily in Arles by

---

[96] On this rendering of *lenta voce*, see *TLL* VII. 2, col. 1165, lines 21–30, and Löfstedt (1950), 81–2.

[97] As he also said in *Serm.* 47. 5, Caesarius here criticizes the belief that there was a "third place," a purgatory, between heaven and hell. For Caesarius's beliefs on the subject, see Jay (1957).

[98] The sin of *infidelitas* could also refer to breach of promise, disloyalty, or treason.

the holy man. One of his officials came forward and began to criticize him by saying, "Lord, let these captives go through the streets and beg for their food, because if they are fed today as they have been by the church, you will not have [any grain] tomorrow from which to make bread for your own table." Then he confidently entered his cell, and as he always did, he sought the aid of prayers, which he never wanted anyone to see. (He used to object strongly if anyone happened to see him stretched out on the ground praying.) He then requested the Lord to provide for the wretched. And he wept so profusely that he immediately obtained what he had asked for. He came out of his cell joyfully and confidently and reproached his official's lack of faith. He then gave an order to the venerable priest Messianus, who was a notary at the time: "Go into the granary and sweep it out so well that, if possible, no grain remains there. Then have bread made as usual, and let us all eat together. And if there is nothing to eat tomorrow, let us all fast, provided that today well-born people and the rest of the captives not go through the streets to beg while we eat and look on." Then calling one of us he whispered in his ear, "Tomorrow God will provide, because he who gives to the poor will never be in need." Indeed, it was still not permitted for these captives to return to their homes.

9. What more [is there to say]? What he ordered was fulfilled. There were complaints, however, from all those supported by the church, who asked what they would eat the next day. But the one who provided a widow for Elijah, so that he might be sustained somewhat by visiting her [cf. 1 Kgs. 17: 9–16], without doubt also assisted Caesarius when he prayed. As a result he always became richer by giving everything to captives and refugees and by reserving nothing at all for himself. The next day, while those supported by the resources of the church anxiously feared the sunrise and awaited the outcome with great trepidation, Gundobad and [his son] Sigismund, kings of the Burgundians, sent before dawn three of the large ships they call *latenae* filled with grain, for they knew how readily the servant of the Lord performed works of mercy.[99] And when all those who from lack of faith

---

[99] This event occurred between 508, when the siege of Arles was lifted, and 516, when Gundobad died. The Burgundians may have sent this gift in gratitude for Caesarius's help in releasing Burgundian soldiers captured in the aftermath of the siege.

had feared the danger of famine the day before saw that the Lord never abandoned his servant, they kept thanking God joyfully for assisting them at a time of need.

10. Now at another time, when the Goths they call Visigoths were lying in ambush, the patrician Liberius[100] was pierced in the abdomen by a lance that penetrated his vital organs. Because this attack occurred across the Druentia river,[101] he remained alone while everyone else, after recovering from the confusion, pursued his assailant. Thoroughly terrified by the danger of his wound and despairing of hope for his life, he fled on foot to the opposite bank, a distance of at least 500 paces [740 meters] and perhaps more, as far as a person can go until he finally becomes weak from loss of blood. But when he reached Saint-Gabriel and could be met by the people of the village, he fell down and lay there utterly without any hope or breath of life. Almost the whole city knows these details, but our information comes from the distinguished Liberius himself, who related his story with tears and great admiration for the powers of the holy Caesarius.

11. Then, he says,[102] Liberius said to us, "In my last moments nothing else came to mind except to proclaim tearfully, 'All these remedies have failed; ask my lord Caesarius to come to my assistance.'" We know from the speed of the messenger that this was true. Caesarius meanwhile, since he had wanted to rest a little in a property of his holy monastery and set some matters in order, began to take care of his busi-

---

[100] Petrus Marcellinus Felix Liberius was designated a patrician by king Theoderic in 500 and served as praetorian prefect of Gaul between 510/11 and 534. See *PLRE* II, 677–81, and O'Donnell (1981).

[101] Despite having the same name in Latin, this was not the modern Durance, which is located some 18 km north of Saint-Gabriel, too far to correspond to the distance of 740 m given in the text. See further Barruol (1969), 238.

[102] I read *inquit* for *inquiunt*, since a plural verb would contradict the indication of a single first-person narrator (probably Messianus) at the end of II. 11 ("as I said above"). The error is understandable. At some stage in the transmission of the text, a copyist mistakenly took the word *nobis* ("to us") to refer to Messianus and Stephanus, which it sometimes does, and changed the original *inquit* to *inquiunt*. In fact, however, *nobis* would seem to refer to Messianus and the others who heard Liberius tell his story ("those of us who were present," II. 12).

ness there. Behold, suddenly a messenger came in breathlessly and humbly asked, "Come quickly, lord. Your son asks that you see him before his death." And although the man of God did not want anyone to depart from this world without the remedy of repentance, he especially did not want Liberius to depart without this remedy. Therefore we immediately went to Saint-Gabriel. As I said above, I shall relate some of the many things that Liberius himself told me.

12. Now Liberius was lying there so close to death that he did not recognize not only the rest of his men, but also his wife or his only daughter.[103] Then he swore that he seemed to hear a man's voice speaking softly in his ear, which said, "Look, the holy bishop is coming." "At that announcement," [he said], "I opened my eyes immediately and knew that the servant of Christ himself was coming. When he approached me, I began to kiss his hands profusely, which I had to do since I had lost all hope of life. Then—I think because of the inspiration of God in me, a sinner—I seized the cloak of my lord and put it on my wound. When I had held part of his clothing there for a little while, the blood, which had not stopped flowing at all, finally ceased. At that point I regained not only health but also great strength, and had I been permitted, I would have tried to hurry back to the city on horseback." Those of us who were present can vouch for the truth of what he said.

13. Now Agretia, the most illustrious of women and Liberius's wife, was troubled by the same affliction as the woman who touched the bottom fringes of the Lord's clothing [Matt. 9: 20]. Because she was similar in faith and devotion, she also was freed [from her affliction]. When I came to meet her, she graciously greeted my humble self and revealed her infirmity to me with the modesty appropriate for a married woman. After calling on the Lord as a witness, with many prayers she demanded that I bring her a piece of the bishop's clothing that had come into direct contact with his skin. And although I could easily have carried out her wishes when I was in the blessed man's cell, I nevertheless began to fear that I would commit the sin of theft [in providing her with] the remedy she was seeking for herself. I therefore

---

[103] Liberius's wife was Agretia, as we learn in II. 13. The name of his daughter is unknown. See *PLRE* II, 36.

indicated to the chamber servant in charge of his sacred apparel that someone had piously asked to be given a small bit of his clothing. For this reason he did not hesitate to give me an old piece.

14. Lord Jesus Christ, you are glorious among your saints, and who is like you? Yet you promised that if anyone believed in you, he would himself do the works that you do. As it happened, it was already quite late when I finally received the scrap of cloth that I was to take away, and it was his custom before going to sleep to put on cloths that had been warmed at the hearth and to set aside those he took off.[104] His servant therefore presented the clothing he thought he would need. But he said to his servant, "I do not want those, but that one and that one." Other old pieces were presented. "The one I am looking for," he said, "is not here." The reason he was searching for it, which he was not accustomed to do, was to reveal what he foresaw in the spirit. Then from his commands his chamber servant and I began to understand that our theft could not be hidden from the servant of God. This happened so that your servant, Lord, could clearly say to us unworthy men, concerning the gifts you had assigned to him, that "someone touched me" [Luke 8: 46]. Then, he said,[105] I was fearful and trembling at what had been done, Lord Jesus, and I began to speak to your servant as if on behalf of the woman whom you cured through your servant's prayers. I said, "Forgive me, lord. I have the piece you are looking for. Your daughter—" Up to this point he permitted me to speak, but then he shushed me and said, "Quiet!" Reverently taking hold of yet another piece of clothing he gave it to me and said, "Go and take both of them to the basilica of lord Stephen, and put them under the altar; leave them there, and in the morning take whichever one you wish to the woman who asked you for it, and bring the other one back to me." I did just as he ordered his unworthy servant to do, and he never asked me to whom I took it, nor did he ask for the clothing back.

15. Meanwhile Agretia kept demanding constantly that I bring her what she had sought. Seeing me coming from afar she stretched out her hands before I could give it to her. She quickly came up to me ready to

---

[104] According to J. Mabillon, these were square cloths applied to the abdomen for warmth, d'Achery and Mabillon (1668), 672, note a.
[105] This is Stephanus again.

snatch what I was delivering. Before I could take the little cloth out from under my cloak where I was carrying it, she hurried with the eagerness of faith to take what she had demanded. After I had taken out the little cloth, I gave it to her. She paid it reverence by looking at it and kissing it devoutly, as was proper. Then she put it around herself over her clothing. There was no delay: with the Lord's assistance the consequence of her faithful petition was immediately apparent. Through the bishop's clothing the Lord's servants already had [in his lifetime] what they are known to have after his death. At last, as she herself used to tell the story, when she had placed the piece of clothing to her chest, all her limbs and nerves were immediately gripped by a shivering attack, not particularly painful, which made her body shake considerably with fear and trembling, as usually happens when people are sprinkled with cold water. But the Lord's mercy was immediately present there, and the flow of blood ceased and never again returned to her. And the saying was fulfilled in her: "Go, daughter, and let it be done for you in accordance with your faith" [Matt. 8: 13; 15: 28].

16. It happened one time that four or five bishops came to meet him. He went down with them to the basilica of St. Stephen for Vespers. When the service had been completed and he had given his blessing to the people, a woman came up to them in the audience chamber as they were leaving. She had incurred a sickness so terrible that day and night her hands unceasingly struck one another, as though they were rolling something. She cried out tearfully, "Lord Caesarius, have pity on a wretched person. Pray that I might regain control over my hands." As was his custom he prostrated himself in prayer with the other bishops. When each had risen, he nodded to one of the holy bishops and said, "Please lord, I ask you, make the sign of the cross over this woman's hands." He obeyed most dutifully, but the aforementioned woman's hands continued to twitch as before. Crying out more forcefully she said, "Lord Caesarius, I call upon you, I ask you. You make the sign of the cross." Again he prostrated himself in prayer, and after rising made the sign of the cross over her afflicted hands, which immediately stopped twitching. The woman then left in good health, giving thanks to God and to the holy man.

17. Now when he came each year to bless the oil for the catechu-
mens in the baptistery, and [later] when he sat down in the small
apse[106] to bless the newly baptized,[107] little boys and girls sent by
their parents with small vessels of water and oil for him to bless were
always running around eagerly. And when those carrying vessels and
flasks ran into one another in front of the congregation, the sound of
objects striking [the ground] was heard and seen, and yet the glass in
which the oil consecrated by Christ's servant had been poured was never
broken.

18. Once while he was visiting parishes, we came to a fortified
place called Luco.[108] There was a woman there named Eucyria, who
presented her slave girl and prostrated herself at his feet. She tearfully
begged him to pray to the Lord for the girl. He in turn examined her
case, since he was a man full of God and very thorough in every respect. He asked what infirmity she had. They replied, "A demon the
peasants call Diana. The girl is so possessed that she is regularly
beaten [by the devil] almost every night. Often she is even brought
into church between two men to ensure that she stays there. She is so
painfully afflicted in secret with diabolical lashes that her crying is
heard continuously, and she is not able to respond at all to those who
are close to her."

19. Then at the demand of all those who accompanied Christ's
servant, they asked to visit her so that the truth of the matter might become apparent. Lord Caesarius therefore allowed holy Lucius, a priest,
and Didimus, a deacon, who were at that time going around the parishes
with him, to hurry and see her in private. I too went in obedience to
these men. If the faithful believe me, I say in God's presence that I saw
with my own eyes that the blows she had received on her back and
shoulders several days before were beginning to heal. The fresh blows
received the day and night before, however, were mixed among them.
At this point she was again presented to Caesarius, and she appeared so

[106] For *cocumula* I read *conchulam* with Cavallin (1934), 117, n. 4.
[107] As Caesarius points out in *Serm.* 129. 5, *infantes* refers not only to
children but to the newly baptized of any age.
[108] Location unknown. If it was the modern Le Luc (Var), as suggested in
Krusch, 491, n. 1, it was too far east to be situated in Caesarius's diocese.

confused—her eyes disturbed and her face averted from him—that it appeared to everyone that she was unable to look at the face of God's servant. But he placed his hand on her head and gave her his blessing. Then he blessed oil and ordered her to be anointed with it at night. And immediately she became so healthy that she was never vexed by the temptation of the devil again.

20. On another occasion when we had come into a parish, a child of about eight years came onto the altar in clerical dress.[109] After the sermon—which the bishop did not hesitate to deliver himself from memory not only in the city but also in all parishes whenever he could—when he had gone back to the altar from the chancel, he began to celebrate the Mass. The child, however, began to be seriously troubled by a very wicked spirit. Trembling and foaming at the mouth he was shaken in a terrifying way. Then a great terror seized us all. Caesarius raised his eyes to heaven, and prayed to the Lord for a cure. Then, ignoring the child, he returned to saying the Mass. A priest named Ursus from the [parish] church of Berre then put the child at Caesarius's feet. Reluctantly taking up the child Caesarius said, "May God pardon you, blessed man. This is a task for others, not me." And although he refused in order to avoid human arrogance, divine power was nonetheless made available to God's servant. When the boy was put at his feet, he immediately got up healed. No wicked spirit ever returned to him; indeed, I later saw him as a subdeacon in the same church.

21. Now when he had come to visit the parish of La Ciotat,[110] the daughter of a man named Novatus had apparently incurred a new kind of demon. It was so wicked that any time she put her foot outside the door of her house, a flock of crows immediately rushed into her face and tore it apart. And when she had been shaken with fear and was wallowing in foaming [blood], they disfigured every part of her body that they found uncovered, that is, her face, neck, or whatever else they found. When she was presented to the holy man, we saw crows come all the way up to the basilica that she had entered and in which the man

---

[109] Junior clerics of this age were not uncommon in Gaul. Their duties were normally to sing or read in church, Beck (1950), 52–3.
[110] For *Cytharista parrochia* as La Ciotat, see Rivet (1988), 201.

of God waited. They flew around it at a distance, but even then they were not shameless enough to dare to fly inside. Now when she had come before him, and he had seen her face lacerated and deformed, he said to us in private, "Never have I read of, seen, or heard of a demon of this kind attacking anyone." Then in front of the holy altar, he placed his hands over her head, blessed oil, and anointed her eyes and ears. With everyone watching she returned down the street to her home in good health. She came to the church during the two days we were there, and was never assaulted after that.

22. Some time later, he said,[111] Caesarius came to a property belonging to our church, where the parish of Succentriones is located.[112] A bath house had been built there with high walls. If anyone at any given moment happened to go by it, he would immediately be called by name. At the same instant he looked with fear at huge stones falling in front of his feet or behind him. Everyone was careful never to go past the place. For this reason they would also warn everyone who did not know about the place not to go there lest they come to harm.[113] And when—mark this!—the man of God had been summoned to another church and was traveling there, the cleric whose responsibility it was to carry his staff forgot it. This was the duty of his notaries, in which capacity my useless self was serving. When the inhabitants of the place found it, they joyfully proclaimed that it had been furnished to them by their lord so that they could find something belonging to him. They were amazed and thanked God and hung the staff from the wall. And immediately the devil's snare was put to flight, and until the present the adversary has not dared to inflict any more wicked evil on anyone in that place.

23. It also happened one time that a man came from [northern] Gaul, Benenatus ["Well-born"] in name but not in deed. He complained that he and his grandchildren were captives. He had a young girl whom

---

[111] Messianus takes up the story.

[112] Location unknown. Baths could be found in towns, wealthy villas, or large villages, for example, the village of Saint-Jean-de-Garguier in the diocese of Arles, *CIL* XII. 594; Benoit (1936), 5–6.

[113] Demons were widely thought to inhabit abandoned bath houses. See further Bonner (1932).

he had dressed in boy's clothing and showed to Caesarius. "This is my grandson," he said, "and with me and his sister, who is hurrying here after us, he is detained as a captive. Then the man of God, grieving over their captivity, acted in accordance with the affection that the Lord had inspired in him from infancy. He greeted each of them politely and kissed them, the man who introduced the girl and the girl whom he believed was a boy. When he had given each of them ransom money, they returned to the place where they were staying.

24. Two days later the bishop called the girl back, this time in her own clothing, so to speak, to give her more *solidi*. In doing this he was following the suggestion of Jacob, a holy man and priest, who asserted in his holy simplicity that Benenatus's complaints were all true. Then Benenatus received ransom money for this child, that is, for the girl, a second time. But those who were concerned about the case realized that on the second occasion he was introducing the same girl he had first displayed in male clothing. I indignantly mentioned this to the holy man of God, as did Jacob, with some embarrassment. But since he was always very mild and kindly toward strangers, he said to the priest, "Do not become angry, holy man. You have done well to commend a stranger. God will reward you for your good intentions. And may God pardon that wretched man for his sin in making me kiss the girl. And may the girl be rewarded for daring to kiss a bishop, albeit an unworthy one. Let God make her such a good nun that she never kisses another man." But because God, as judge of future events, doubtless knew that she would not be able to maintain her virginity, she immediately departed from this world the next day, so that the prayer of God's servant would not go unanswered. These deeds are very well known in Arles at the basilica of the Apostles, where [Jacob] lived.[114]

25. On another occasion a woman in Marseille happened to dislocate her foot so badly that for a long time she could not put it on the ground. Held up by the hands of her slaves and enduring great pain, she could barely be led to church. But because the Lord's mercies are numerous, he produced reasons for the man of God to go to Marseille

---

[114] The location of this basilica is unknown.

when he wanted him to. When she learned of his arrival, the woman had herself brought to meet him. Although she received a prayer and a blessing from him, she did not dare to mention her own affliction to him, but as she left him, she asked to be permitted to approach his saddle horse. She faithfully touched the injured spot with the saddle cloth that was covering the saddle. Immediately she recovered her former good health, as if she had suffered no affliction. Unimpaired, she returned home on her own feet with no one supporting her and has given thanks to the Lord to this very day.

26. One day in this city—something that many know—the house of a man named John that was next to the [women's] monastery caught fire. The fire then began to come so close that no one doubted that everything there would surely be burned up. Disturbed because they were forbidden to leave the monastery, the maidservants of God threw their books, their possessions, and themselves into cisterns where, by God's mercy, to keep them from despairing, there was no water at the time. The assistants [to the steward][115] of the monastery ran to the father of the nuns and announced that the fire was already near their cell. Caesarius quickly ran out in the middle of the night along the wall to the place where the fire was approaching. Throwing himself forward in prayer he gave them orders and shouted from the wall, "Do not fear, blessed women." Soon, burning with the flame of his own virtue he sent the fire away.

27. Nor shall I be silent about the following very well-known event, which is said to have occurred once in the Alpilles. Constant bad weather kept destroying the property of a certain very noble man. The rain was most destructive, and powerful hailstorms devoured all the produce of the area. Every year, therefore, there was no hope of assistance for the place. It then happened again that Caesarius's staff was left there by accident. From this staff the owner ordered a cross to be made. Fortified by his faith, he then put it up in a prominent place, so that the staff of the disciple and the cross of the master might counteract the incoming hailstones. In honor of his servant, God deigned to work

so great a miracle there that after he had driven away the bad weather he made the place very fertile.[116]

28. Likewise one day the house of a man named Vincentius caught fire. Its wooden terrace was overcome by flames. Seeing that he could do nothing Vincentius went as fast as he could to the lord. Throwing himself at his knees he asked him to say a prayer. Caesarius went outside and made the sign of the cross against the flames. They retreated and were extinguished so quickly that no sign of them appeared on the planks of the terrace.

29. A certain priest also informed us recently that some years earlier when he was still a layman, his daughter was harassed by a demon. In sorrow and mourning he asked one of his friends, "What should I do? I am unhappy because my daughter is afflicted by a demon. It would have been better for me if she had never been born or if she had died." His friend responded, "Do not weep, but go and take her to lord Caesarius, and present her to him in private, and he will cure her." He did not hesitate, but came to Arles and met him on his journey. Prostrating himself at his feet, he said tearfully, "Lord, take pity on me in my wretchedness. Cure my daughter." Caesarius carefully asked what she had, and he responded, "A demon." Then he said to him, "Keep silent and go back home. In the morning, when Matins are said, come back and bring your daughter with you along with her mother. After Matins, wait in the vestibule of [the church of] St. Stephen. And when you see that no one else is about, come to my cell and call me." He did just as Caesarius ordered. Caesarius then came out without anyone's knowledge. He knelt on the ground and prayed with the girl's father and mother. Then he rose, made the sign of the cross over her, and sent her away in good health.

30. Another time while walking down a street in the city he saw from the opposite side of the forum a man possessed by a demon. When he had noticed him from afar, he held his hand under his cloak so that he would not be seen by his own attendants and made the sign of

[116] For the power of the cross to work such miracles, see Flint (1991), 188–9.

the cross in the man's direction. Immediately the man was freed from
the enemy's attack.

31. How holy and sweet it was when day by day, unceasingly, he
preached the word of God, welcome to those who wished to hear it and
unwelcome to those who did not [2 Tim. 4: 2].[117] Now whenever he
went to bed late, which he did so as not to keep away from the divine
scriptures and holy instruction even at that hour, he used to say to us,
"Tell me. What have we dined on today? What sort of dishes have we
had?" We remained silent and sighed, for as he often did, he was guid-
ing our reasoning to the point where he could elicit from us what he
wanted to say about spiritual food, and it was for this reason that he
questioned us. He said again, "I know that if I asked you what we ate
for dinner and even what you had for the afternoon meal, you would remember.[118] But if we asked what was read at table, you would not remember. From this it is to be understood that we remember what
tastes good to us. But we do not remember what not only seems in-
sipid on the palate of our heart but perhaps even disgusts us." And
groaning deeply he used to say, "The failure to remember what is good
is indeed unfortunate. Nothing is more unfortunate than this!"

32. And then he used to repeat from the beginning what had been
read or explained, and he used to say to us poor wretches in a sorrowful
and prophetic voice, "Gather in the Lord's wheat, gather it in, because I
tell you truly, you will not have a long time in which to do so! See
what I say. Gather it in because you will be searching for that time;
truly you will be seeking those days and you will long for them very
much." But even though at that time we did not take this seriously because of our sluggishness, nevertheless we now realize that what he said
has come to pass. That saying of the prophet was fulfilled in us: "I
shall send you a famine in the earth, a famine," he says, "not of bread
and water but of hearing the word of God" [Amos 8: 11]. Although the
sermons he produced are still recited, that unceasing voice has nonethe-

---

[117] Cf. *Serm.* 1. 3; 4. 2.

[118] Monks and nuns in Arles normally ate two meals per day (Caesarius,
Regula virginum 71). The exact times of these meals normally varied by
day and by season. While Caesarius's rules do not state these times, *Regula
Benedicti* 41 gives abundant details. See further, Biarne (1981), 107–15.

less ceased, which fulfilled the saying of the prophet, "Cry out unceasingly" [Isa. 58: 1]. He said this often: "When someone's palate despises the word of God, his soul grows feverish. When he regains his health, then he will hunger and thirst for what he scorned and refused while sick."

33. Who could ever explain in words the sweet and holy dessert[119] [we had after dinner]? The servant of Christ, he said,[120] used to say to us, "We have now completed dinner to the best of our ability." But it was suggested by those standing nearby and by his chamber servants that he rest on account of his weariness. For having grown tired he was hardly able to breathe. He answered, "You are right to say so, but wait a little while." Then his chamber servants said, "Lord, why do you say 'wait'? You have grown weary by speaking a great deal at the table, and up to this point you have not kept silent. Rest for a little while now." He answered again very pleasantly, "You are right to say so, but because we have completed dinner, will we prepare no dessert?"

34. Because he is aware of unknown things, he knows what I am saying. For when the Holy Spirit had begun to speak through him, he revealed everyone's vices so clearly that we might all recognize ourselves. He beat us with the lashes of his instruction and promptly restored us to good health by anointing us with divine medicines. Like a holy and spiritual instrument-player he touched the chords of each man, so that when we went away from him we loudly resounded inside with what he had said. "Lord," we said, "each and every one of us thanks you. [I thank you] because I am no longer mindful of my injury, nor am I angry with my brother. For what your servant preaches is certainly true, and I prefer to suffer evil than to have the holy man put on the stand on Judgment Day to testify against me." One of us said the same about pride, another about anger, and yet another spoke in the same way about the vice he was troubled with. Our souls refreshed and restored to health, we all went back to bed giving thanks to the Lord.

---

[119] Although *reticinium* usually means a light afternoon meal or snack (Krusch, 496, n. 4), it seems here to mean a (spiritual) dessert, since it takes place after dinner.
[120] Stephanus resumes the narrative.

35. Who can ever describe, good God, holy creator, what sort of expression, what sort of appearance, what sort of character [he had]? Holy father, we miss your instruction, your beauty, your expression, your character, your knowledge, and the charm you (among others) had as a special gift from the Lord. How holy was your life, how pure and sweet your compassion! Lord Jesus, who can even imagine, let alone explain in words, how numerous and how wonderful were your gifts? For when he proceeded to bless the baptismal fonts—if those who saw him also hear what I am saying, they are credible witnesses for themselves, because they trust their own observations—who ever believed that he was an earthly man in that procession? Lord God of heaven, I say in faith and truth that throughout the forty years he was bishop, whoever saw him in procession on that day saw him as if they had never seen him before, so new did he appear in everyone's eyes. His face shone brightly along with his soul, because in fact his life improved so much through continual successes that he always became better than he was before. Thus whatever happened within himself fittingly appeared on the exterior.

36. Because of this not only were there visions of various saints, but even more impressive is the fact that the Lord Jesus with all his disciples revealed himself to him in a vision. He did not boast of this far and wide, nor was he exalted in spirit, but he admitted it to only one trustworthy individual, who swore an oath that he would keep silent. It is this individual who asserts in God's presence that the vision occurred. Moreover, two years before his death Caesarius was shown in spirit all the [blessedness] prepared[121] in heaven which he would receive for all his works, and it was said to him, "Rejoice in the Lord, for behold what you will receive for your service!"

37. Because there are still quite a few important matters which we are passing over in order to avoid prolixity, most of those who share this knowledge with us will no doubt be sorry that we have passed over the many stories that we know in common. We ask that they pardon us, for it is quite unsuitable and burdensome either for a barbarian to presume to speak at length to a learned audience or for an inarticulate

---

[121] For this Christian sense of *praeparatio*, see *TLL* X. 2, col. 750, line 84 – col. 751, line 5.

person, when he cannot speak, to want to mutter any further. May God grant that our composition comes to an end before the love, the nurturing, the charity, the preaching, and every holy memory of our lord and your holy father come to an end in our hearts.

38. Nevertheless, I shall also relate in brief the miracles his relics performed after his death, but before this account was written.

39. For a long time Desiderius, the public archivist, suffered so much from a quartan fever that he even lost the strength of his youth.[122] Then he drank some of the water in which Caesarius's holy corpse had been washed. He was immediately cured so thoroughly that not only did the fever not attack the young man again, but by the Lord's favor he even regained his strength and previous vigor.

40. The son of the illustrious Salvius[123] was very seriously afflicted by a tertian fever. It was his desire to try to cure his son with the repeated potions recommended for this illness, but nothing at all could help him. Then, like a Christian man, he said to his son, "Go and either find the water with which [the body of] the lord bishop was washed or wash relics of his clothing and drink that water, and the Lord will heal you." When this was done, all fever and misfortune immediately departed from him.

41. The son of the illustrious Martianus, now deceased,[124] was also so seriously afflicted by troublesome fevers that even his doctors despaired of the case. But since gracious God inspires those whom he wishes to heal, he promptly and confidently asked that a piece of clothing from God's servant be given to him, so that he could wash it and drink the water. [He ordered his servants] to run to me and to others not present who had reserved a piece of this clothing for themselves. What he sought was found at someone's house. A piece of it was presented

---

[122] For the continuity of records and record-keeping in the late Roman world, see Posner (1972), 205–23. Desiderius is known only from this passage, *PLRE* II, 356.
[123] Known only from this passage, *PLRE* II, 974.
[124] Known only from this passage, *PLRE* II, 730.

to him. He drank the water and was healed. He is still alive, himself a witness of this miracle.

42. Another time when I was going down the street, a Frank was walking in front of me completely bent over and trembling from the chills of a quartan fever. When I decided to walk quickly where I was going [and passed him], he shouted after me, "Blessed man, if you have any, give me some of the clothing of St. Caesarius. Since it works on many afflictions, I want to drink some, because I have the chills." In a hurry to get where I was going, I said, "If you wait for me, I will give you what you ask for tomorrow." He replied, "I have time today, and I am already trembling all over. When will I have time to wait for you?" Then, reflecting that it was not in vain that he had on so many previous occasions been placed before me in the street, I said to him, "Come young man. I will give you what you seek." Immediately we both returned. When we had entered my cell and washed our hands, I brought forth the linen cloth with which the holy corpse of our dear lord had been wiped dry. I then took a very small part to give him. But the Frank said to me angrily, "Take it away, man, why are you deceiving me? I heard that the blessed man used not linen but rags. I want to wash these and drink them in water." I replied tearfully, "You are right; you have heard the truth. But the saint's body was cleansed with this when he died." And he said, "Give it to me if I am to be healed." He took [the linen cloth] and immediately received good health from the Lord.[125]

43. No tongue can adequately recount the benefits that Christ provided to bodies and souls through the prayers of the Lord's servant. Although my rustic speech sounds clumsy because I am not an eloquent speaker, nevertheless when wise men speak, even a few testimonies are of great advantage.[126] Those who receive true sayings with a faithful mind have their own senses for proof.

44. Be that as it may, I should not pass over what recently happened when his body was in repose in the cell from which he had made

---

[125] For *acceptum* I read *accepto*, and for *sensit* I read *recepit*, following Cavallin (1934), 94.
[126] For this translation of *emolumenta rerum*, see Cicero, *De officiis* III. 36.

his heavenly ascent. In the presence of the holy brothers who were reciting verses of the psalms[127] there, one of his chamber servants was adjusting a lamp, which slipped from his hands onto the floor. It neither turned over nor broke nor was extinguished.

45. Now while this evangelist, as we read, carried out his outstanding and very important work of the word, "welcome and unwelcome" [2 Tim. 4: 2], and while he fulfilled his holy duty, there appeared in Arles, with tranquillity and peace and by God's consent, the kingdom of the most glorious Childebert, a most catholic kingdom in Christ's name [536/7].[128] The bishop did not betray the city as the Arians charged, but rather prayed constantly for all. Childebert's kingdom is gentle in its virtue, even-handed in its severity, and conspicuous in humility. It does not terrify the bishops of the Lord with fear but restrains them with veneration. It is outstanding to everyone in Gaul and fair to all in the church, humanely showing its benevolence[129] by virtue of its majesty.[130] Refreshed and delighted by this the man of God despised the threats and constant accusations of the mad Arians, which had been falsely made up. "He saw," therefore, "and was gladdened" [John 8: 56], "and he was placed next to his ancestors in good old age" in the name of Christ, "full of days" [Gen. 25: 8].

46. He then entered the seventy-third year of the course of his entire life, during which the cycle of his episcopacy had turned into its fortieth circuit.[131] When frequent illness made him appear feeble, he realized through the Spirit that the day of his death was imminent.[132]

---

[127] For this translation of *capitella*, see Agde (506), can. 30, *CCSL* 148 (1963), 206.

[128] Childebert obtained control over Provence from Vitigis, king of the Ostrogoths, in return for a promise of military assistance against the emperor Justinian, who sought to recover Italy for the empire. See further James (1988), 95–6.

[129] For *civitatem* (which appears to be a misprint), I follow Krusch: *civilitatem*.

[130] For this translation of *privilegio celsitudines*, see Cavallin (1934), 118–19.

[131] He was thus seventy-two years old, and had served thirty-nine years and some months as bishop.

[132] Premonitions of death are a standard feature of death scenes in hagiography. For this and related *topoi*, see Scheibelreiter (1984).

In the midst of the considerable pains from which he suffered he inquired how near it was to the date of the burial of the most blessed Augustine.[133] When he learned that his feast day was near, he said, "I believe that the Lord will not separate my death much from his. For as you yourselves know, I have loved his most catholic way of thinking by as much as I differ from him in merit. Nevertheless, I do not think that the day of my burial will be very much separated from the time of his death." Meanwhile the departure of Israel from the land of Egypt, that is the departure of the bodily life of a holy soul from this world, became imminent and drew near.

47. He therefore ordered that he be carried by his attendants on a sedan chair into the monastery of virgins that he had founded. He went to console the anxious women who were not sleeping because of their suspicion that he was about to pass away and who were forgetting to eat. The sound of psalms had been stifled by their tears, and they were producing groans instead of song and lamentations in place of alleluias. But even then, when he had consoled and addressed his daughters, he did not bring joy but increased their sadness, for indeed, it was easy to see that their kindly father was now about to go to his heavenly reward. Then in his usual charming way he addressed the venerable Caesaria [the Younger], mother of over two hundred girls, and he consoled her and urged her to strive for the reward of her celestial vocation. And he warned them to hold fast to the Rule which he had established so many years earlier. After this[134] in his testament he also commended the women to the bishops succeeding him; through his letters [he commended them] to the rest of the clergy, the office of the prefect, the counts, and the citizens so that they might suffer no hardship at all in future times.[135] His monastery had at that time been established for a full thirty years. He then said a prayer for them and gave them his blessing, saying farewell for the last time. While the women continued their weeping, he returned to the church.

---

[133] Augustine died and was buried on 28 August 430.
[134] For *sequenti* as a synonym for *postea*, see Cavallin (1934), 120.
[135] That is, Caesarius commended the women to the entire city, which was made up of the clergy, royal officials, and the lay population. For the office

48. Now on August 27 [542], the third day after the feast of St. Genesius,[136] the day before the feast of the death and burial of St. Augustine the bishop, and the day after the anniversary of the dedication of his monastery,[137] since he had already said farewell to everyone the day before, Caesarius happily dispatched his blessed spirit to Christ at dawn. He died in the arms of the bishops, priests, and deacons who were in attendance.

49. The clothes on his sacred corpse were snatched away with such pious violence by various mourners[138] and members of the faithful that we priests and ministers who were in attendance could hardly remind them to wait patiently to receive the relics. From these relics, as I have said above, cures of the sick are with God's power repeatedly celebrated in unbroken succession. Caesarius was the cause of admirable rejoicing in heaven but on earth left behind intolerable grief, shared not only by the good but by any evildoers who might have been watching as well. For what citizen or foreigner, because of his tears, sang a psalm at his funeral? But everyone—good and evil, just and unjust, Christians and Jews,[139] those leading and those following the procession—called out together, "Woe, woe, and more woe each day, for the world was not worthy to have such a herald and intercessor any longer."

50. And so he was buried in the basilica of St. Mary which he himself had built, where the holy bodies of the nuns from his monastery are buried. We too with faithful devotion and the zeal that he deserves venerate him on earth, whose soul we trust in, praise, and glorify because it shines in heaven.

The end

---

of the prefect (governor) of Provence and the Frankish counts, see James (1988), 182–91.

[136] A martyr and the earliest patron saint of Arles. His feast day was 25 August.

[137] 26 August 512.

[138] Boglioni (1979), 203, suggests that these were professional mourners, on the grounds that they are listed separately from "members of the faithful."

[139] For this *topos* of inclusion, see Blumenkranz (1949).

THE TESTAMENT OF CAESARIUS
INTRODUCTION

At his death in 542 Caesarius left behind a will drawn up in the form of a letter and addressed to the local clergy, Caesaria the Younger, and his nunnery. Unlike the wills of other Gallo-Roman aristocrats such as bishop Remigius of Reims,[1] the main purpose of Caesarius's will was not to transmit his personal property—of which he owned very little (*Test.* 4)—but rather to confirm certain arrangements that he had made during his lifetime on behalf of the monastery. The first set of arrangements was made to ensure that after his death the institution would remain free from interference by his successor. Caesarius therefore requested and received from pope Hormisdas certain privileges of autonomy that sharply restricted episcopal involvement in the monastery's affairs (*Letter* 18). The second set of arrangements was intended to endow the growing community with adequate funds for the support of its members and the upkeep of its property. Because he had so little wealth of his own to bestow on his foundation, Caesarius had made use of the wealth of the church for this purpose. With special grants of exemption from popes Symmachus and Hormisdas for what the Roman church had recently deemed an illegal procedure (*Letters* 7b, 15, 18), Caesarius succeeded in transferring church wealth to the monastery in the form of guaranteed revenues from some church properties and the outright ownership of others. Fearing that after his death these arrangements would be altered by his successor or (less likely) by the institution itself, Caesarius designated them both as heirs and proceeded to use his will as a vehicle for making provisions which they were legally obliged to respect.

The exact date of the will is now impossible to determine, since the day and the consul's name promised in *Test.* 2 are not preserved by any surviving manuscript. The document appears, however, to have been composed in stages, beginning with a version composed before the dedication of the monastery in 512.[2] This early version was then

---

[1] Ed. B. Krusch, *MGH SRM* III (1896), 336–9. On its authenticity, see Jones, Grierson, and Crook (1957).

[2] As indicated by the future perfect verbs in *Test.* 1 ("the whole congregation which the Lord will have gathered there") and *Test.* 10 ("If, however—

68 TESTAMENT OF CAESARIUS

revised—perhaps several times—to take into account changes in the monastery's situation. It was presumably the last of these revised versions that was preserved in the monastery after Caesarius's death. Those of its provisions that could still be read, with crosses marking illegible passages,[3] were eventually copied into a charter issued in 992 by count William I of Provence to reconfirm the monastery's privileges. Although this manuscript was seriously damaged by an inept attempt at restoration around 1730, and was finally destroyed along with the monastery during the French Revolution, it remained intact long enough to be copied several times. It was on the basis of these copies, particularly the copy made by Jean Raybaud in 1718, that the first good text of Caesarius's testament was established by Morin in 1899.[4] Two editions of the *Testament* have subsequently been published, by Morin in 1942[5] and de Vogüé in 1988.[6]

The timing of Morin's first edition of the *Testament* was inspired by an attack made on its authenticity three years earlier by Bruno Krusch.[7] He first maintained that the document did not meet the legal standards for a will, since it was composed in the form of a private letter rather than as a public act registered in the city archives. He also asserted that in denying that he had received any wealth from his parents (*Test.* 4), the author of the testament contradicted a passage in the *Life* which stated that Caesarius was born of noble parents (I. 3). He finally argued that in stating that the monastery would be "under the authority of the bishop of Arles, as the canons stipulate" (*Test.* 3), the testament contradicted the provisions of *Letter* 18. According to Krusch, the *Testament* of Caesarius was not a genuine attempt by Caesarius to protect his foundation, but rather a forgery sponsored by one of his successors to legitimate control over the institution.

In arguing for the authenticity of the *Testament*, Morin demonstrated that contemporary wills could be composed in the form of letters, showed how Caesarius, though born of noble parents, had re-

---

God forbid!—the congregation will not have been established there"); see de Vogüé–Courreau, 362–4.
[3] de Vogüé–Courreau, 375.
[4] Morin (1899).
[5] Morin II, 281–9.
[6] de Vogüé–Courreau, 379–97.
[7] Krusch, 450.

nounced his wealth upon entrance into the local clergy, and explained the way in which Hormisdas's letter still allowed for the monastery's subjection to the local bishop.[8] In addition, by using the same techniques he was beginning to employ in editing the sermons of Caesarius, Morin was able to show that many turns of phrase in the will were characteristic of Caesarius's style.[9] Krusch quickly accepted these arguments and affirmed the authenticity of the *Testament*, which has not been questioned since.[10]

In form if not in substance the *Testament* is typical of Merovingian wills, which continued to follow most of the conventions of Roman wills.[11] Because it was composed as a letter, the document opens with epistolary rather than testamentary conventions: the bishop's name and title, the names of his addressees, and a salutation. This was followed by a conventional declaration of the testament itself ("I have by the grace of God composed my will"), together with the confirmation of the testator's signature and date, both now unfortunately missing, and a much abbreviated version of the "codicil clause." In the following paragraph the will turns to its most important function, the institution of heirs, in this case, the women's monastery and the bishop of Arles, whose role was to assume the sum total of the testator's rights and responsibilities. This is followed by a standard disinheritance clause and by a formula directing the heirs to carry out in general such provisions as legacies and manumissions.

The remainder of the will is concerned with specific testamentary provisions. These include legacies of clothing, slaves, and land to heirs and other beneficiaries, as well as the confirmation of provisions made during Caesarius's life for the property, revenues, and privileges of the monastery. It is these provisions that constitute the will's particular interest, for they provide concrete evidence of the mishaps Caesarius feared might befall the institution after his death and the precise efforts he undertook to ensure its survival and success.[12] With the conclusion

---

[8] Morin (1899), 108–112.
[9] Ibid., 106–108.
[10] *MGH SRM* IV (1902), 770.
[11] On the formal characteristics of Merovingian wills, see Nonn (1972), which I have followed closely. On Roman wills generally, see Nicholas (1962), 234–70.
[12] Klingshirn (1990), 460–4.

of these provisions the will ends abruptly without any of the customary closing formulas, the date and place at which the document was drawn up, or the signatures of Caesarius, his witnesses, or his notary.

The edition used for this translation is de Vogüé's, whose notes and translation have also proven helpful. Numbering of sections is based on Morin's edition. In translating the *Testament* I have attempted to convey its meaning as clearly as possible without minimizing its difficulties, which result not only from the imperfect state of the text but also from lost details of ecclesiastical and monastic property holdings, obscure references to local topography, and the uncertain history of the schemes Caesarius employed for enriching and protecting his foundation.

THE TESTAMENT OF ST. CAESARIUS

1. Peace to the church of Arles. Bishop Caesarius to the priests and deacons; to the holy and venerable abbess Caesaria [the Younger], whom the Lord, through my humble self, has put in charge of our monastery; and to the whole congregation which the Lord will have gathered there by his grace: eternal salvation in the Lord God!

2. Since the piety of the church makes it customary to bestow the assistance of its largesse on pilgrims and the poor, and rightfully so, how much more should it open its heart in goodness and mercy whenever the opportunity or necessity arises to bestow its gifts on holy and God-fearing people? And so with this letter, which I have confirmed by the signature of my right hand, and to which I have added the date and the consul's name below,[1] I have by the grace of God composed this my will. I have signed it in my own hand and have also confirmed it as a codicil by the praetorian and civil law.[2]

3. When I Caesarius, a sinner, will have repaid the debt owed by human flesh, let the whole monastery of St. John in Arles, which I founded, be under the authority of the bishop of Arles, as the canons stipulate.[3] And I wish and order that it be my heir. In addition, I designate the bishop of Arles as co-heir with my monastery.[4] Let all other

---

[1] These are missing from the document.

[2] This is a shortened version of the formula by which a testator declared that if his will was deemed invalid for any reason, the dispositions it contained would still be valid as a codicil. A codicil was not an addendum, as in modern legal parlance, but an alternative and less formal instrument of succession. See Nicholas (1962), 270.

[3] Chalcedon (451), can. 4, 8, ed. N. P. Tanner, *Decrees of the Ecumenical Councils*, I (London and Washington, D.C., 1990), 89, 91; Agde (506), can. 27, *CCSL* 148 (1963), 205. This canonical authority was severely circumscribed by Pope Hormisdas' grant of immunity in Caesarius, *Letter* 18. On the relationship between monasteries and bishops in Gaul, see in general McLaughlin (1935), esp. 129–40.

[4] I read *Arelatensem episcopum coheredem meo monasterio*, Morin (1899), 101, lines 20–21. All MSS and editions place this sentence just before the last sentence of §3. Nonn (1972), 72, has argued, however, on the basis of a study of the formal elements of Merovingian wills, that statements establishing heirs belong in the *institutio heredis*, rather than in the *caput*

heirs or heiresses be disinherited. Anything I have given to anyone before or through this will of mine or have bequeathed or have ordered to be given, let it be given. Any men or women I have ordered to be free, let them all be free.

4. Since I own nothing of my parents' property, it is not without a feeling of shame that I have so boldly produced this my will. Nonetheless, I am compelled by the thought that some religious individuals, fearing the uncertain day [of death], have piously made donations to my church. I wanted therefore to make this my will, so that after my death none of my kinsfolk would presume to disturb the church over which I preside, except in connection with the gifts I gave them in memory of myself. In this will, I wish and order that none of my kin presume to seek anything from the monastery or the bishop of the church of Arles except that which I have given them.

5. To my lord the holy bishop who worthily succeeds my unworthy self: although everything is in his power, nevertheless, if he orders it and considers it right, let all the paschal vestments that were given to me be of service to him, together with the better quality shaggy cloak, the better quality tunic, and the thick cloak, which I have left behind. As for the rest of my clothes, except for the hooded cloak, let my clerical and lay attendants divide these among themselves, with the favor and permission of the lord bishop if he so commands and makes a gift of them. I confirm the gifts that I previously conveyed to the monastery. And if I have bestowed anything on anyone by a motive of piety, either by letter, written conveyance, or orally, I wish it to be valid. Regarding the cell in the courtyard of St. Stephen, on the right as you enter, which the subdeacon Augustus of blessed memory occupied, I ask the lord bishop to deign to grant it by perpetual title to the stewards of the monastery in order to protect their reputation, so that the stewards

---

generale, where this statement appears. While Nonn argued on these grounds that the passage was an interpolation made for the benefit of Caesarius's successor to the detriment of the monastery, I would argue that the passage was merely misplaced. I have therefore restored it in the translation to what I take to be its proper position. See further Klingshirn (1990), 461.

of the monastery who succeed them might have it.[5] And I particularly wish and so ask the lord bishop that the holy congregation have no one as steward for the monastery or as priest for the church of St. Mary except whom it has chosen for itself and has sought to have appointed.[6]

6. And although I shall take for granted your piety, lord bishop, nevertheless, in the fear that you might by chance adopt the dangerous suggestions of others to the detriment of my monastery, I entreat you earnestly by the Father, the Son, and the Holy Spirit, and by the fearful day of the Last Judgment that the old enemy may never prevail over you in such a way that you allow your servants to be unjustly saddened or that you permit any of the possessions that I have bestowed upon them to be taken away from them. For by God's favor I have not, without discretion and justice, sold ecclesiastical property with direct title[7] to any lay persons whatever, except for property of little use to the church and unprofitable. Please see to it therefore that what I have assigned to these holy souls dedicated to God with the consent and signature of my sacred brothers remains theirs with permanent title.[8]

7. And I entreat you, my noble daughters, by the holy and inseparable Trinity and by the Second Coming of our Lord Jesus Christ, to direct your requests respectfully, as if through the Lord, to the bishop who by the will of God worthily succeeds my unworthy self. Esteem him with a pure heart, and do not sadden him by your disobedience. For I trust in God's mercy [that it will deign to inspire] all bishops to weigh out for you with a pure love what has been brought by the pious, so that they permit you to lack nothing that is necessary for bodily sustenance.

---

[5] The steward of the monastery (*provisor*) was responsible for maintaining its physical links with the outside world, such as distributing alms to the poor (*Regula virginum* 42) and bringing in workmen (*Regula virginum* 36). On efforts to insulate the sisters from their stewards, see *Regula virginum* 36, 39.

[6] For the burial church of St. Mary, see *Life* I. 57. The nuns also had the right to choose their own abbess, *Regula virginum* 61.

[7] For this translation of *ius directum*, see *CTh.* X. 1. 2, and *TLL* V. 1, col. 1254, lines 28–33.

[8] That is, in accordance with Agde (506), can. 7, 45, *CCSL* 148 (1963), 195-6, 211.

8. I ask you again and again, holy bishop, through divine grace, that above all you treat the monastery of holy virgins as having been entrusted to your very great care, and that you very kindly allow the community of these women to be provided for. And if anyone wishes to give you bad advice, dutifully answer that arrangements that were made or granted with the advice of a bishop not only should not be reversed but cannot in any way be reversed. And especially because the holy popes of Rome have also [confirmed] this by their authority,[9] do not let me believe this of you, my holy lord bishop. For an unfair suggestion can never acquire so much support from you that against the lawful will of a bishop, of whatever quality I may be . . .[10] [For] through my efforts, the wealth [of the church] has increased a great deal for you: it has almost doubled. In addition, through my humble self merciful God has for the most part granted immunity from taxation [to the church] not only in the immediate vicinity of the city and within it but also in the suburban villas.[11]

9. We have preserved [the estate called] Ancharianum[12] for the most part, although we gave a small parcel of it to the monastery. [Of the estate] we have kept [for the church] approximately 100 *aripenni* of vineyard[13] and fields of 300 *modii*,[14] and [have granted] 100 *modiatae* of

---

[9] *Letters* 7b, 18.

[10] There is a lacuna at this point.

[11] Immunity from taxation was reportedly granted to the church of Arles by Alaric II, although the authenticity of the passage is in doubt. See *Life* I. 20 with note 30.

[12] The names of Roman estates in Provence were often formed by the addition of *-anum* to the family name of a past owner, in this case a certain Ancharius, Rostaing (1950), 367–8, 390. The location of this estate is unknown.

[13] The *aripennus* was a Celtic measure of area (= Fr. *arpent*) equal to 50 Roman *iugera* (Columella, *De re rustica* V. 1. 6), or about 33 $^1/3$ acres.

[14] This figure measures the area of land by the amount of seed with which it was customarily sown, since the *modius* was a measure of volume. Assuming that the land was planted with wheat, and assuming a rate of 5 *modii/iugerum* which Palladius gives for *triticum* or *far* (*Opus agriculturae* XII. 1, ed. R. H. Rodgers [Leipzig, 1975], 216), 300 *modii* of seed would suffice for 60 *iugera*, or about 40 acres.

land to the aforementioned monastery.[15] [Those] which I planted comprise 40 *modiatae*,[16] and from the old vineyard we have given barely 30 *aripenni*.[17] To support the virgins we have reserved the following properties for this holy church: Gallicinianum,[18] Neocleanum,[19] and The Twins,[20] with their ponds and marshes, and all rights and boundaries; the pasture in the Stony Field,[21] and any others there might be; the field in Triple Spring[22] on the Fortified Road, and any others there might be; and Ornedum,[23] Martinatis,[24] The Grove,[25] and Missianianum,[26] with all the pastures and marshes they possess, and all rights and boundaries.[27]

10. Holy bishop, I therefore earnestly entreat you that if almighty God should give any greater gift to this holy mother church and to the monastery of holy virgins through the generosity of those who fear him, your holy love not detach one from the other. If, however—God

[15] The *modiata* was the amount of land customarily sown with 1 *modius* of grain, *TLL* VIII, col. 1227, lines 61–4. At 5 *modii/iugerum*, 100 *modiatae* equalled 20 *iugera*, or about 13 $^1/_3$ acres.

[16] 8 *iugera*, or about 5 $^1/_3$ acres.

[17] 15 *iugera*, or about 10 acres.

[18] Named after a Gallicinius, the site may be Saint-Césaire-de-Gauzignan (Morin II, 288), 17 km west of Uzès. Its location outside the diocese of Arles demonstrates the extent to which diocesan landholding could reach beyond the diocese itself.

[19] Named after Neocles; location unknown.

[20] *Gemellis*, which Morin II, 288, identifies with Gimeaux in the Camargue, 4 km southwest of Arles.

[21] This is La Crau, the large rocky plain stretching east of Arles.

[22] *Trifontio*, which Morin II, 288, identifies with Le Trébon, a northern suburb of Arles on the road to Saint-Gabriel.

[23] Poly (1976), 82, n. 27, identifies this with Ulmet in the Camargue, 24 km south of Arles.

[24] Some estate names were formed by the addition of the suffix *-atis* to a personal name; this estate was named after a certain Martinus, Rostaing (1950), 429–30. Its location is unknown.

[25] *Silvam*, which Morin II, 288, identifies with Sylvéréal, located 27 km southwest of Arles along the petit-Rhône.

[26] Morin II, 288, identifies this site, named after a Missianius, with Méjanes on the Etang du Vaccarès, 16 km southwest of Arles.

[27] That the abbey still possessed many of these properties in the ninth century and beyond demonstrates the practical value of Caesarius's will. For details see Poly (1976), 82.

forbid!—the congregation will not have been established there, or if perhaps later after being established—may this not happen!—it will have ceased to exist, these gifts should revert to the mother church. I have written this only to put my fears to rest. Far be it from me, most pious bishop, to fault you for inattention to the fact that, as I have said above, divine piety has through my humble self permitted an immunity of so many headings of tax liability[28] to be given to the church.

11. I confirm through this my will what I have given to the monastery with the consensus of my brother bishops. I wish your servant, the abbess Caesaria [the Younger], to be given what she made, the larger cloak that she made from the thick cloak. I wish a towel to be given to my lord Leo the priest. I wish a cloak and the better quality belt to be given to my lord bishop Cyprianus. I confirm through this my testament whatever I have given to my slave Bricianus. Let Agritia, my slave girl, very willingly serve the monastery of the holy abbess Caesaria [the Younger].[29] I also confirm the orchards I have given to them or their relatives. I commend all my domestic servants to you, lord bishop, in the presence of God and his angels.

[28] *Capita* could also be translated "shares of landed assessment." On this difficult technical term, see Goffart (1974), 131, n. 26.
[29] It might not be a coincidence that Agritia the slave had the same name as Liberius's wife, *Life* II. 13–15. It is possible that she was owned by the noble Agritia, from whom she received her name. She may then have been presented to Caesarius as a gift. *Regula virginum* 7 prohibits individual nuns from owning slaves in the monastery, but does not rule out the monastery's corporate ownership of slaves. There were certainly slaves in Radegund's monastery for women, which followed Caesarius's *Regula virginum*, Gregory of Tours, *Hist.* X. 16.

THE LETTERS OF CAESARIUS
INTRODUCTION

Although Caesarius must have written many letters in his lifetime, only seven have survived: one each to his sister Caesaria the Elder, Ruricius of Limoges, and Agroecius of Antibes; two to pope Symmachus; and two to the bishops of Gaul. Two other letters sometimes attributed to Caesarius have been proven spurious: a letter to Caesaria the Younger (*O Profundum*), which may have been written by his nephew Teridius,[1] and a letter to Caesaria the Elder (*Coegisti me*), which was composed in the seventh century.[2] Besides the letters Caesarius himself wrote, fifteen letters written to him have also survived. These include four letters from his fellow aristocrats and churchmen Magnus Felix Ennodius, Avitus of Vienne, and Ruricius of Limoges, and eleven letters from the bishops of Rome. With the addition of three letters written by the bishops of Rome to the bishops and churches of Gaul on topics of direct concern to Caesarius, the total comes to twenty-five, small in comparison with the letter collections of churchmen like Sidonius and Ennodius—but of precious value for our understanding of Caesarius's links with the world outside of his diocese.[3]

All but one of these letters are translated here. The exception is Caesarius's encyclical letter to the bishops of Gaul, conventionally referred to as *Sermon* 1, which Mueller translated with Caesarius's other sermons. With the exception of *Letters* 18 and 21, this translation is based on Morin's text. His system of enumeration has also been used, but with important modifications. *Letters* 7, 8, and 14 in Morin, each of which consists of two separate documents, have been divided into parts a and b. In addition, letters that Morin published outside the letter collection, which he did not number as letters, have been arranged in chronological order and designated *Letters* 18-21. Numbering of paragraphs within letters is based on Morin's paragraph divisions.

---

[1] de Vogüé–Courreau, 402-4.
[2] Etaix (1975), 211-18.
[3] For a survey of letter collections in southern Gaul and the links of family and friendship they represented, see Mathisen (1981).

THE LETTERS OF CAESARIUS

Letter 1
Magnus Felix Ennodius to Caesarius
513

Born to an aristocratic family in 473/4, perhaps in Arles where his relations were still living in Caesarius's time, Ennodius was raised in Pavia, where he entered the service of bishop Epiphanius in 493. At Epiphanius's death in c.496 he moved to Milan, where he was ordained a deacon by bishop Laurentius. During his years in Milan Ennodius composed most of the works for which he is remembered: 297 letters, the *Life* of Bishop Epiphanius of Pavia, the *Libellus pro synodo* written for pope Symmachus at the time of the Laurentian schism, a panegyric to Theoderic, an autobiography, and assorted rhetorical pieces, hymns, and poems. The success of his writings and political activities was eventually rewarded with an episcopal see. At some point between 513 and 515 he was ordained bishop of Pavia, a position he held until his death on 17 July 521.[1]

Ennodius wrote this letter to congratulate Caesarius on his successful appearance before Theoderic in the spring/summer of 513 (*Life* I. 36–38). The letter itself is undated, but it must have been written after Caesarius's visit, that is, in the summer/autumn of 513. This may make it the latest datable letter in Ennodius's collection; the absence of any reference to Caesarius as a brother bishop suggests that Ennodius had not yet become a bishop himself.[2] The letter's mannered, repetitive, and obscure style is typical of Ennodius, whose letters, like those of Symmachus, Sidonius, and other late Roman aristocrats, were intended more to cultivate friendship and reap its benefits than to convey information.[3]

---

[1] For biographical details and a survey of his writings, see Schanz–Hosius IV. 2, 131–48; Fontaine (1962); and *PLRE* II, 393–4.
[2] F. Vogel, *MGH AA* 7 (1885), xxv.
[3] Matthews (1974). On the style of Ennodius's letters, see Fontaine (1962), cols. 400–1, and Dubois (1903).

ENNODIUS TO BISHOP CAESARIUS[4]

You have announced in your letter the outcome for which I had hoped. For as a result of your venerable correspondence I have learned what the heavenly emperor compelled the lord king [Theoderic] to decide in your case. For my own part, after your vindication was disclosed, I did nothing to hide my joy at the result. Who does not know that earthly powers have been subjected to a bishop most noble in Christ's service, and that the power that threatens defendants has been overcome by the protestations of innocence? When has princely purple despised either the monastic habit or the *pallium*?[5] When in the face of Christian humility has the most powerful liberty believed that it was permitted to do whatever it wanted? Or when was it permitted to want something that would cause harm? But if we consider ancient examples in this context, and if you mention the savagery of tyrants[6] toward the worshippers of God, we know that they killed our fellow believers so that [those believers] might never die. At that time the eternal leader brought life and eternity to his soldiers by an obliging sword; they for their part lost their original sin with the help of their enemies. But divine law brought you forth, my lord, into a world that was already Christian, and nourished you with the milk of the apostolic breast. You surpass others just as the concentrated magnitude of the sun surpasses lesser stars. He who has examined you with the eyes of the inner man has learned something. For since even your expression fosters purity, you reproach sinners without speaking. Wherever you go, good people discover aspects to imitate from your way of life; and aspects to be avoided are demonstrated to the wicked. You are blessed, whom God has directed to teach by warnings and examples. As a guide, you always attract others to the pious and straight path. When you are speaking, who does not hope to learn more and gather more? When you turn your talent[7] to books by way of communication, you even instruct teachers. The greatest of writers, whoever he might be, is indebted to

---

[4] In Ennodius's corpus the letter is *Epist.* IX. 33, ed. G. Hartel, *CSEL* 6 (1882), 257–8, and ed. F. Vogel, *MGH AA* 7 (1885), 321.

[5] A reference to Symmachus's conferral of the *pallium* on Caesarius (*Life* I. 42; *Letter* 7b).

[6] By "tyrants" Ennodius means the pagan emperors who persecuted Christians.

[7] For *genius* as *ingenium*, see *TLL* VI. 2, col. 1840, lines 3–4.

you for endowing him with the gift of eloquence. In you the light of word and deed come together. Whence did this privilege come for the people of Transalpine Gaul? Whence did this unexpected loftiness come for my relations [in Arles], to have sent such a man? But why is a heavenly matter being investigated in earthly regions? Could any courtly arrogance not lie prostrate before you? Could it take away what you desired, a man gentler than sheep, whom only errors make aggressive? Your merits and diligence call for a broader treatment from me, but the law of letter-writing curbs my wordiness. In conclusion, kindly accept the gift of my service and recommend me to our God by the approbation of your prayers. Keep me frequently informed about what you are doing or have done. I pray also that you inform me by letter whatever Rusticus's petition moves you to do.[8] As I hear, he dresses up his lovers by calling them "wives" and thinks that a criminal affair can be excused by a legal term.

Letter 2
Bishop Avitus of Vienne to Caesarius
502/18

Born *c*.460 to a powerful aristocratic family of the lower Rhône valley, Alcimus Ecdicius Avitus could boast of many ancestors and relations who had held high office, both secular and ecclesiastical: the emperor Eparchius Avitus, his father Hesychius, and his uncle Sidonius Apollinaris, bishop of Clermont.[9] By 494 Avitus himself had become a bishop, succeeding his father in the see of Vienne. As bishop he played a prominent political role in the Burgundian kingdom, and was himself instrumental in the public conversion of king Gundobad's son Sigismund from Arian to catholic Christianity. Ennodius called him "the most outstanding bishop in Gaul."[10] In 517, a year after Sigismund succeeded his father as king, Avitus presided over the Burgundian council of Epaone. In addition to these pastoral accomplishments he also composed a variety of works, including letters,

---

[8] Rusticus is unknown.
[9] Mathisen (1981), 100; Heinzelmann (1982), 221–2.
[10] *Vita Epiphani* 173.

homilies, theological treatises, a biblical epic in five books, and a hexameter poem on virginity.[11] He died in 518.[12]

In this letter of commendation, typical of the genre, Avitus introduces bishop Maximianus, perhaps the bishop of Trier,[13] to bishop Caesarius. The letter is undated and could have been written at any time between Caesarius's accession in 502 and Avitus's death in 518. In spite (or perhaps because) of the territorial dispute in which the sees of Arles and Vienne were engaged at the time, the tone of the letter is polite and correct.

BISHOP AVITUS TO BISHOP CAESARIUS[14]

Although the venerable letter carrier will ingratiate himself with the affection of fraternal charity, the holy bishop Maximianus nevertheless particularly asked me to send you this letter as a service to him. Its contents make it clear that I ought to be recommended by him rather than he by me. And because he directed me to make his needs known in my own words, I decided to say nothing about his toil in traveling abroad. For, however far in time or distance a bishop has gone from the homeland of his birth, he cannot be called a foreigner where the catholic church can be found. And yet, I should not exaggerate to you the devastation of his region, as though you were unaware of it, since no one who seeks your help, wherever there is distress, is denied access to your compassion. The principal reason for his coming, as far as he has deigned to express it, is that he is seeking a skilled physician somewhere, who cures eye diseases by a skilful remedy. Although the gaze of a religious mind is better occupied in contemplating spiritual concerns and is not excessively terrified about the blindness of the exterior man, Maximianus seeks this cure, as far as I understand it, so that he might try rather to satisfy his friends in their need for this endeavor.

---

[11] Gregory of Tours, *Hist.* II. 34; Schanz–Hosius IV. 2, 382–9.

[12] For biographical details and further bibliography, see Schanz–Hosius IV. 2, 380–2, and Isetta (1983). On Avitus's style, see Goelzer and Mey (1909); on his historical importance, see Burckhardt (1938), Wood (1980), and Rosenberg (1982).

[13] Morin (1935).

[14] In Avitus's corpus the letter is *Epist.* 11, ed. R. Peiper, *MGH AA* 6. 2 (1883), 45, and *Epist.* 9, ed. U. Chevalier, *Oeuvres complètes de Saint Avit, évêque de Vienne*, new ed. (Lyon, 1890), 144–5.

At the same time he does not wish the conduct of his episcopal duties to appear to be reprehensibly diminished through the fault of neglected health. He also seeks the hope of recovering his sight, I think, from the biblical example in which medicine concealed in an angel, namely an eye-salve of bile, brought back our Tobit to the sweetness of health. For because he was blind with regard to earthly affairs but saw what was invisible to the world, he was intent on eternal light and already almost oblivious to the mortal day [cf. Tobit 11: 2–15]. For this reason receive our brother with your customary sincerity and worthy reverence. And convey any consolation that is owed to an anxious man. Our common desire will be fulfilled if some sort of cure heals his infirmity. But certainly if not, at least the eye of a bishop's conscience, unaffected by blindness, might recognize the imperishable expression of another's piety.

Letter 3
Caesarius to bishop Ruricius of Limoges
506

Like his distant relatives Ennodius and Avitus, Ruricius was born into a prominent Roman family in southern Gaul, probably c.440. Sidonius Apollinaris celebrated his marriage to Hiberia in 461/2 by composing an epithalamium.[15] In c.477 Ruricius underwent an ascetic conversion under the influence of Faustus of Riez, and in c.485 became bishop of Limoges. His surviving corpus consists of 82 of his own letters and 13 letters addressed to him. Most were written during his episcopacy to relatives and fellow bishops.[16] Ruricius died c.507.[17]

In this letter Caesarius criticizes Ruricius for not attending the council of Agde in September 506. Although the council had reaffirmed every bishop's responsibility to attend councils or send a representative in his place (can. 35), Caesarius did not invoke the penalty for non-compliance, which was excommunication until the next synod.

[15] Sidonius Apollinaris, *Carm.* X and XI, Loyen (1960), 95-102. For the date, see ibid., xxxiv.
[16] For a literary analysis, see Hagendahl (1952).
[17] Schanz–Hosius IV. 2, 550–1.

This was probably due as much to the thirty-year difference in their ages and to Ruricius's seniority as bishop as to the adequacy of his excuse. These factors also help to explain Caesarius's deferential tone. The letter dates just after the council, to the autumn of 506.

BISHOP CAESARIUS TO THE HOLY LORD RURICIUS MOST DESERVING IN DISPLAYING THE LIGHT OF CHRIST AND MOST PIOUS IN DESIRING CHRIST[18]

While my mind was much troubled about why we did not deserve to have your presence at the synod, my holy lord bishop Verus deigned to inform me that he had sent your letter to me at Agde through his deacon, which I by some accident or fault do not remember having received.[19] Yet I most certainly trust my holy lord and your brother, and I prefer to attribute this to the negligence of the letter-carrier. But although you sent your holy and desirable letter, nevertheless, as you yourself know well, it was very important that you also send a representative to sign in your place and to confirm as your representative what your holy brothers decided. But because I know how holy, how constant, and how pious was your desire to attend, I explained your vow and your holy desire to all your brothers, for which we neither could nor should have blamed your piety in any way. But although we did not have your desirable presence, we nevertheless realized that we deserved the patronage of your prayers. These having been offered, I greet you with due affection and honor, and I ask that you commend me to the Lord by your holy and renowned prayers as well as by your merits. At the same time I mention to your piety that, because your son Eudomius desires, if possible, to work this out, we are also having a synod in Toulouse in the coming year, Christ willing, where if possible he also

---

[18] In Ruricius's corpus the letter is *Epist. ad Ruricium* 12, ed. B. Krusch, *MGH AA* 8 (1887), 274; *Epist. ad Ruricium* 7, ed. A. Engelbrecht, *CSEL* 21 (1891), 448–9; and *Epist. ad Ruricium* 7, ed. R. Demeulenaere, *CCSL* 64 (1985), 402–3.

[19] Verus served as bishop of Tours from 495/6 to 507. He did not attend the council of Agde, but sent his deacon Leo, who signed in his place. It was probably later the same year that he was exiled from his see by king Alaric on suspicion of treason (Gregory of Tours, *Hist.* X. 31), and it may have been at this time that his meeting with Caesarius took place, Schäferdiek (1967), 36–7.

wants the Spanish bishops to convene.[20] And so pray that the Lord might deign to give success to this holy desire of his. I commend to your virtuousness, with my greatest possible warmth, my holy and very sweet brother, the priest Capillutus, your friend and admirer.[21] On his behalf I thank you abundantly and richly, for as he himself declares, your pious and sincere kindness has devoted itself to him more than anyone can say. Now therefore, because he has ardently sought your piety in accordance with your desire [to see him], I have deemed it fitting to have him deliver you a letter from my humble self. When he returns, if Christ should grant this, I long to receive your letter as I would a gift from heaven. Pray for me.

Letter 4
Bishop Ruricius of Limoges to Caesarius
506/7

Despite Caesarius's attempts at deference Ruricius was offended by the brash young bishop's suggestion that he had acted improperly. After elaborating on the excuse for his absence he suggested that Caesarius was himself partly to blame and demanded that in the future his senior rank and age be given the proper respect. This letter also dates from late 506/early 507.

RURICIUS TO MY HOLY AND APOSTOLIC LORD MY BROTHER BISHOP CAESARIUS WHOM I PARTICULARLY ESTEEM WITH ALL HONOR AND LOVE[22]

Our brother and fellow priest Capillutus has appeared doubly pleasing to me at this time, by meeting with me, who have long desired to see him, and by presenting me with your presence in the form of your

[20] Eudomius was a senior official in the Visigothic kingdom, *PLRE* II, 409. In *Epist.* II. 39, Ruricius consoled him and his wife on the death of their son. Because Alaric was killed at the battle of Vouillé in 507 and his kingdom thrown into disarray, the council of Toulouse never took place.
[21] Capillutus was a correspondent and letter carrier of Ruricius; he may have lived in Arles, Ruricius, *Epist.* II. 21, 31, 40.
[22] In Ruricius's corpus the letter is *Epist.* II. 33, ed. B. Krusch, *MGH AA* 8 (1887), 336; ed. A. Engelbrecht, *CSEL* 21 (1891), 417; and ed. R. Demeulenaere, *CCSL* 64 (1985), 371–2.

letter. On his return I took care to send this letter by means of which I repay the duty of charity that I owed to your blessedness. As for your question, why I did not come to the council as our conversation indicated I would, this was due to illness and not to my own wishes. For you yourself can recall how tired I was when you saw me in Bordeaux—and that was in winter, when I am usually stronger than normal.[23] In summer weather I can scarcely tolerate this chronic illness, even in my own home and in cool places. So I admit that I would have been unable to bear the heat of that region, if I had come. I therefore hope all the more that you will deign to pray for me. If you wish me to come at the other time that you announce, providing God has kept me alive, you should indicate this to me earlier through your messenger, because I note that your recent letter came to me very late. Even if it were not for my rank or my age, I should not be informed later than others. Frankly, I should perhaps have been consulted [in advance]. For even if the authority of their cities furnishes others with prestige, the humility of a city ought not to remove my authority, since it is much better and more noble for a city to become well known because of its bishop than for a bishop to become well known because of his city.

Letter 5
Bishop Ruricius of Limoges to Caesarius
502/7

In this letter Ruricius commends his grandson Parthenius to Caesarius on the occasion of his visit to Arles. This was the same Parthenius whose slave Caesarius cured (*Life* I. 49).[24] The letter dates between Caesarius's accession in 502 and Ruricius's death in 507.

---

[23] Caesarius and Ruricius met in Bordeaux during Caesarius's exile there in 505/6, *Life* I. 21–4.

[24] For Parthenius's kinship to Ruricius and his later career, see p. 34 *supra*, n. 69.

BISHOP RURICIUS TO MY HOLY AND APOSTOLIC
LORD AND BROTHER BISHOP CAESARIUS
WHOM I PARTICULARLY ESTEEM IN OUR LORD CHRIST[25]

We who seek occasions for writing to one another out of mutual
love should not ignore the opportunities offered to us, by which,
through the mediating [power] of writing, we confer on one another a
part of our presence. Writing is sent out but is not lost. It is given
away and retained. It seems to depart but does not depart. It is directed
by me and is taken up by you. It is written by me and is read by you.
It is not divided up. Although it seems fragmented, it is nonetheless retained whole in each man's heart. For in the fashion of the divine word
it is handed over and does not leave. It is bestowed on the one in need
and is not taken away from its author. It is a gain for the recipient
without being a loss for the donor. It enriches the needy man without
impoverishing its owner.[26] And so with the arrival of my very dear
grandson Parthenius [in Arles] I did not hesitate to send this letter with
him, so that I might share my presence with you in a letter and commend him at the same time. You should realize that any affection you
deign to convey to him, you are giving me as well. At the same time I
also ask you in particular to pray unceasingly for me and for my children. Let not the distance between our regions hinder our mutual affection. Those who love one another in the Lord, who is present everywhere, must not be thought to be physically separated when they are
mentally joined together in him. Pray for me.

Letter 6
Pope Symmachus to the bishops of Gaul
6 November 513

As a result of bitter divisions within the church, senate, and population of Rome following the death of pope Anastasius in 498, opposing factions elected rival successors to the see of Rome: the priest

[25] In Ruricius's corpus the letter is *Epist.* II. 36, ed. B. Krusch, *MGH AA* 8
(1887), 339; ed. A. Engelbrecht, *CSEL* 21 (1891), 421–2; and ed. R.
Demeulenaere, *CCSL* 64 (1985), 375–6.
[26] Up to this point the letter is identical with Ruricius, *Epist.* II. 5, addressed to Namatius, the father-in-law of one of his sons. On Ruricius's
fondness for "plagiarism," see Hagendahl (1952), 12–31.

Laurentius and the deacon Symmachus. The resulting "Laurentian schism" continued for eight years until king Theoderic permanently resolved it in favor of Symmachus. But even after the formal resolution of the dispute the divisions it had exposed in Rome and the Roman church did not disappear, and Symmachus spent much of the rest of his pontificate trying to restore his reputation and rebuild the consensus he needed, both at home and abroad.[27]

When Caesarius traveled to Rome in 513 (*Life* I. 42), one of the subjects of his conversation with pope Symmachus was the status of his ecclesiastical province. After the Visigothic conquest of Provence in 476/7 the Durance river was established as the boundary between the Burgundian kingdom to the north and the Visigothic kingdom to the south. Because civil boundaries normally determined ecclesiastical boundaries, the metropolitan province of Arles was split in half, and the bishop of Vienne began to exercise metropolitan control over eleven dioceses north of the river that the bishops of Arles claimed as their own on the basis of pope Leo's settlement of 450.[28] At some point between 496 and 498 pope Anastasius approved this *de facto* arrangement,[29] but Symmachus rejected it in 500, albeit with no practical results.[30] The change from Visigothic to Ostrogothic control in 508 did not resolve the dispute, since the border remained in the same place as before. Caesarius therefore raised the question again in 513. Eager to gather outside support for his primacy, Symmachus reconfirmed pope Leo's decision of 450 along with his own ruling of 500. But it was probably not until 523, when an Ostrogothic army annexed the territory north of the Durance, that Caesarius could finally exercise jurisdiction over the entire metropolitan province that he claimed as his own.

---

[27] The *Liber pontificalis* contains two accounts of these events, composed in the 530s and 540s; both are favorable to Symmachus. Another account, favorable to Laurentius, is contained in the so-called Laurentian fragment, composed in the 510s. All three accounts are translated in R. Davis, *The Book of Pontiffs (Liber Pontificalis to AD 715)*, 43–6, 97–9, and 101–2. See also Caspar (1930–3) II, 87–129; Richards (1979), 69–99; and Moorhead (1992), 114–39.
[28] *Epist. Arel.* 13, ed. W. Gundlach, *MGH Ep.* 3 (1892), 20–1. For a full discussion of the controversy, see Mathisen (1989).
[29] *Epist. Arel.* 23, ed. Gundlach, 34.
[30] *Epist. Arel.* 24, ed. Gundlach, 34–5.

The inflated style and imperious tone of this letter are typical of papal correspondence from the period.[31]

SYMMACHUS TO HIS MOST BELOVED BROTHERS, ALL THE BISHOPS SERVING IN GAUL[32]

1. The praiseworthy traditions of the apostolic see induce us to maintain constant watch over the harmony of the universal church, which now extends over the whole earth. The church grows even more powerful if a later age reverently observes what the fathers have established. When he was presented at the threshold of the church of the blessed apostle Peter, my brother and fellow bishop Caesarius, bishop of the metropolitan city of Arles, requested that I reaffirm in my own words the long-established privileges of the churches [of Arles and Vienne]. Through its reliable teaching the Roman church therefore confirms everything that our predecessor, pope Leo of blessed memory, decreed concerning this dispute between the churches of Arles and Vienne. To prevent forgetfulness, the perpetual enemy of truth, from being able to prevail, and to prevent the vigor of an earlier decree from declining into feeble old age by the long passage of time, I have thought it necessary to shed light again through my pronouncements on papal declarations promulgated long ago.

2. Therefore, in just the same way as our predecessor pope Leo, having acquainted himself with the allegations of the parties involved, once defined which dioceses were to be assigned to the bishop of Arles and which to the bishop of Vienne, I too decree that his definition is not annulled by [one bishop's] usurpation [of the other's dioceses]. But as I said before, in accordance with the grant of the aforementioned pope Leo, the bishop of Vienne may claim for his own jurisdiction the cities of Valence, Tarantaise, Geneva, and Grenoble. And he should not contemplate seizing anything more than what was once granted him by the apostolic see. The bishop of Arles in turn should control according to his privilege and honor all other dioceses and parishes in the future. By

---

[31] Schneider (1954), cols. 582–3.
[32] In Symmachus's corpus the letter is *Epist.* 14, ed. Thiel, 722–3. It is also *Epist. Arel.* 25, ed. Gundlach, 35–6.

this observance a reverence for tradition is maintained, and episcopal glory is further raised up from humility.

3. Accordingly, dearest brothers, [bishops] should be content with their own portion of honor and should not unlawfully presume to exceed the boundaries of power granted to them, either through secular patronage or through presentation of any other excuse. Indeed, each one of you ought to be zealous to acquire grace through devoted service rather than incur divine displeasure and human envy through ambition. The obligation of supervision entrusted to me does not permit me to be silent. So let us rejoice at those who persevere in the harmony of the apostolic see by complying with ecclesiastical rules, and let those who refuse to follow catholic teaching admit that they are separated from the grace and love of the church. Most beloved brothers, may God keep you safe. Issued November 6 in the consulship of the most distinguished Probus [513].[33]

Letter 7a
Caesarius to pope Symmachus
513

On his visit to Rome Caesarius also presented Symmachus with a written petition listing four violations of church law he wanted the pope to condemn.[34] His choice of topics reflects both his interest in church reform and more specifically his concern for the financial security of the monastery he had recently founded. The fact that all of these practices continued to be condemned by Merovingian councils and reformers like Gregory the Great illustrates the limited success of

[33] By the fifth century it was normal for the eastern and western emperors to designate one consul each; beginning in 480 barbarian kings took over the naming of the western consul. The "ordinary" consuls they named assumed their duties on January 1—one in Rome, the other in Constantinople—and provided their names to the year. Although the year was formally named after both consuls, western documents were usually dated only by the name of the western consul. For details, see Bagnall et al. (1987), 13–35.

[34] The absence from the petition of the name of a letter carrier (cf. *Letter* 8a) suggests that Caesarius presented the document to Symmachus himself.

Symmachus's response. This petition is known only from the copy reproduced at the end of *Letter* 7b.

COPY OF THE PETITIONARY LETTER[35]

1. Just as the papacy has taken its beginning from the blessed apostle Peter, so it is necessary that your holiness clearly show by appropriate teachings what customs the individual churches ought to observe.

2. Some people in the province of Gaul are alienating ecclesiastical estates by titles of different kinds.[36] In so doing they diminish on the strength of their own judgment the resources allocated for the needs of pious donors and the poor.[37] I request that the authority of the apostolic see prohibit this from happening except perhaps in cases where a gift is to be bestowed on monasteries in consideration of piety.

3. I likewise request that no layman who has exercised jurisdiction in public office or has governed provinces on behalf of any ruler be ordained a cleric or bishop unless he has for a long time lived the way of life prescribed by law and his life has been examined.[38]

4. As for widows who have already worn a religious habit for a long time, and nuns who have already been in monasteries for a long

---

[35] In Symmachus's corpus the letter forms part of *Epist.* 15, ed. Thiel, 727–8. It is also *Epist. Arel.* 27, ed. Gundlach, 40.

[36] In general the alienation of church property by any kind of transaction, whether by sale, donation, or exchange, was prohibited by canon law, although exceptions were often made. See Agde (506), can. 7, *CCSL* 148 (1963), 195–6.

[37] In Caesarius's view both donors and the poor benefited from the practice of charity: donors received spiritual rewards and the poor material rewards. See *Serm.* 27. 3.

[38] Such candidates for the higher clergy were expected to renounce further sexual relations with their wives, if married, and adopt an ascetic style of life, Agde (506), can. 16, *CCSL* 148 (1963), 201; Epaone (517), can. 37, and Arles (524), can. 2, *CCSL* 148A (1963), 34, 43–4.

time, I also request that no man be permitted to marry them even if
they are willing or to abduct them against their will.[39]

5. I suggest this also in my humble petition, that no one be
permitted to attain the episcopate through bribery, and that no one hire
powerful people as their supporters by paying money.[40] To guard
against this more easily, neither clerics nor citizens should presume to
promulgate a decree [of election] without the knowledge and consent of
the metropolitan bishop.[41]

6. Prohibit all these irregularities from happening by your power
of castigation, so as to preserve both in your church and in the
aforementioned province a moral teaching conducive to good actions.

Letter **7b**
Pope Symmachus to Caesarius
6 November 513

SYMMACHUS TO HIS MOST BELOVED
BROTHER CAESARIUS[42]

1. The reasonableness of your request encourages us to assent
gladly to the wish of your brotherhood, because the various points you
ask the apostolic see to confirm do not deviate from the caution and
foresight of the fathers. And although ecclesiastical regulations
comprehend almost everything, we do not believe it superfluous to
repeat afresh what has often been prohibited.

---

[39] Abduction was a common means of forcing a woman (or more often her
parents) to agree to a marriage. Many women, of course, had entered monastic life precisely to escape unwanted marriages. See Rouche (1987), esp.
469–73, and Wemple (1981), 149–74.

[40] For the role of bribery and patronage in episcopal elections, see Dalton
(1927) I, 288–300.

[41] The decree of election, called a *consensus*, was a document indicating the
approval of the clergy and people for an episcopal candidate. For details,
see Claude (1963), 22 ff.

[42] In Symmachus's corpus the letter is *Epist.* 15, ed. Thiel, 723–7. It is
also *Epist. Arel.* 26, ed. Gundlach, 37–9.

2. We do not permit possessions that anyone has willingly given or left to the church to be alienated by titles or contracts of any kind or for any reason, except perhaps in cases of convincing necessity, when they may be bestowed on clerics for their merits, on monasteries in consideration of their religious way of life, or certainly on pilgrims. This must be done in such a way, however, that the recipients use these possessions not perpetually, but temporarily for as long as they live.[43]

3. We strongly issue this reminder, that those who try to enter the episcopate through bribery, by the promise of ecclesiastical goods rather than by God's grace, should not succeed in their desires. Let them either restrain themselves from impulses of this kind, or realize that they will without doubt suffer canonical penalties.

4. As for lay persons, we decree that they should not be permitted to enter the episcopate easily. Times and ranks have been established for them by which they ought to aspire to this status.[44] For whoever is promoted without due process easily inspires ill will, and without the appropriate experience he cannot be officially elected.

5. We detest the abductors of widows and virgins because this crime is so heinous. We prosecute even more vigorously those who have tried to marry virgins dedicated to God, whether they are willing or unwilling. We order such men suspended from communion for the atrocity of this very wicked crime.

---

[43] This answer must have disappointed Caesarius, for it allowed monasteries to receive only the usufruct, rather than the outright ownership, of church property. It was in fact more restrictive than the regulations adopted by the council of Agde, which had permitted alienation in cases of necessity and where small properties of low value were involved, can. 7, 45, *CCSL* 148 (1963), 195–6, 211. Symmachus's ruling was based on the strict limits on alienation the pope had promoted at the council of Rome in November 502, in part to absolve himself of the charge made by supporters of Laurentius that he had unlawfully alienated church property. See further Moorhead (1992), 120.

[44] That is, minimum age limits and the sequence of clerical offices from the lectorate to the priesthood.

6. Moreover, we do not permit remarriage for widows who have long lived according to religious vows. Similarly, we prohibit marriage for virgins who have lived their lives for many years in monasteries.

7. No one should be permitted to acquire episcopal office through bribery. Since this error is condemned in the lay life, who doubts that it would bring indelible scandal to the religious who serve God? No one who desires to become bishop should pay money and hire powerful persons as supporters. Nor should he by spreading any kind of fear intimidate clerics or citizens into signing a decree of election for him or bribe them by offering gifts. Without the presence of a visitor no one should prepare a decree by whose testimony the consent of the clergy and people can be declared.

8. And so we urge everyone to preserve these regulations faithfully and devotedly out of consideration for the catholic religion and the peace of the churches. There is no doubt that transgressors of these edicts will be excommunicated in accordance with the venerable canons.

9. We would like these matters to be brought to the attention of all the bishops.

10. May God keep you safe, dearest brother. Issued November 6 in the consulship of the most distinguished Probus [513].

11. We have granted to your charity alone the right to use the *pallium* throughout the whole of Gaul.[45]

Letter **8a**
Caesarius to Pope Symmachus
513/4

Caesarius complains in this letter that the bishop of Aix was unwilling to accept his metropolitan authority. This dispute had its roots in the fifth-century expansion of the ecclesiastical province of Arles.

[45] For the *pallium*, see *Life* I. 42.

Since Arles was located in the civil province of Viennensis, it should strictly speaking have served as an ecclesiastical capital in only that province. Aix on the other hand, as civil capital of the province of Narbonensis II, should have functioned as its ecclesiastical capital as well. That it did not was the result of the political successes of the bishops of Arles in the fifth century, who had usurped metropolitan control over the provinces of Narbonensis II and Alpes Maritimae alike.[46] In protest against this irregularity the bishop of Aix refused to acknowledge Caesarius's metropolitan authority. Like *Letter* 7a, this letter is known only from Symmachus's response.

COPY OF THE PETITIONARY LETTER[47]

The apostolic see claims primacy for itself over all the bishops of the churches that extend over the whole world, and conciliar decrees make its pre-eminent authority even stronger. For these reasons, by wisely using its power it ought to preserve undisturbed what it granted long ago. In order to enjoy its privileges the church of Arles now makes its petition known through bishop Caesarius and it asks your authority to confirm the power it has had up to this point. May the authority of your blessedness even now confirm by its own precepts what the holy see once ordered preserved by perpetual decree and what was specially ordained by imperial decrees.[48] In particular, advise the bishop of Aix to be warned by the decrees of your holiness that when the metropolitan bishop of Arles has called him to a council, or when divine religion demands his presence at an ordination, he not refuse to come. Under your leadership may the regulations sanctioned over the long centuries by the authority of the ancients be maintained untouched for the present and the future. Petition presented by the abbot Egidius and the notary Messianus.[49]

---

[46] For the background, see Mathisen (1989), esp. 22–5.
[47] In Symmachus's corpus the letter forms part of *Epist.* 16, ed. Thiel, 729. It is also *Epist. Arel.* 29, ed. Gundlach, 42.
[48] For instance, Valentinian III in 445 supported pope Leo's general claims to primacy by declaring "that the bishops of Gaul and other provinces are not permitted to attempt anything against traditional custom without the authority of the venerable pope of the eternal city," *Nov.* 17, ed. T. Mommsen and P. Meyer, 101–3.
[49] Egidius is unknown; Messianus is Caesarius's biographer.

Letter 8b
Pope Symmachus to Caesarius
11 June 514

In his response, written a little over a month before his death, Symmachus confirmed Caesarius's claims to metropolitan control over the bishop of Aix. Ten years later bishop Maximus of Aix signalled his acceptance of these claims by signing the signature list at the council of Arles (524) with the rest of Caesarius's suffragan bishops. Symmachus also used his letter to spell out Caesarius's responsibilities as papal vicar of Gaul.

SYMMACHUS TO HIS MOST BELOVED
BROTHER CAESARIUS[50]

1. He who preserves the venerable regulations of the fathers shows himself a friend of perfect religion. And he who takes care not to leave room for deviations [from these rulings] demonstrates a regard for the goodness of grace. It is reasonable for the holy church of Arles to enjoy its own privileges. Recent audacity should not dishonor what tradition has preserved and the authority of the fathers has confirmed. This should be done in such a way, however, that the privileges acquired over time by other churches are not weakened, since it is not possible for something that involves the injury of the whole to be healthy on its own. Leaving in effect those privileges granted to individual churches by the rulings of the fathers, we have decided that the expertise of your brotherhood should watch over religious matters that arise in Gaul and Spain.[51] And if logic demands the bishops' presence, let each one be summoned by your authority and meet according to custom. And if by God's help a pressing controversy is resolved, let us attribute this to his favor. Otherwise, you should bring the matter still under dispute to the apostolic see, so that when everything has been resolved under its direction, the enemy of goodness might not be able to find an opportunity to please himself.

---

[50] In Symmachus's corpus the letter is *Epist.* 16, ed. Thiel, 728–9. It is also *Epist. Arel.* 28, ed. Gundlach, 41–2.

[51] "Spain" here probably refers to Septimania, the portion of southwestern Gaul held by the Visigoths.

2. Therefore, as we said above, long-standing privileges preserved in individual churches should be maintained. And if the bishop of the church of Aix or any other bishop refuses to obey the metropolitan bishop when he has been summoned in accordance with the canons, he should realize that he will have to undergo ecclesiastical discipline, something we do not wish to happen.

3. Finally, we want you to be especially careful in this respect, that if anyone finds it necessary to come to us on church business from Gaul or Spain, he should notify your brotherhood before undertaking the journey.[52] In this way his honor will not suffer any affront out of ignorance, and we will be able to confidently admit him into the favor of communion without any uncertainty. May God keep you safe, dearest brother.

4. Issued on June 11 in the consulship of the most distinguished Flavius [Cassiodorus] Senator [514].[53]

Letter 9
Pope Hormisdas to Caesarius
514/23

A week after pope Symmachus's death in July 514 his deacon Hormisdas was elected bishop of Rome, as expected.[54] He announced his election to Caesarius in a letter of which only the following fragment has been preserved, appended to a copy of Caesarius, *Letter* 8a.

---

[52] The traveler would then be issued a formal letter of introduction to the bishop of Rome. On the early fifth-century origins of these *litterae formatae* in Arles, see Mathisen (1989), 50.

[53] Flavius, the family name of the emperor Constantine, had become an honorific title in the later empire. It was not used with an aristocrat's full name but was normally appended to his "last" name in the fashion of the English "Mr.," Bagnall et al. (1987), 36–40. Cassiodorus, whose full name was Magnus Aurelius Cassiodorus Senator, was thus designated Flavius Senator.

[54] Caspar (1930–3) II, 129.

HORMISDAS TO HIS MOST BELOVED
BROTHER CAESARIUS[55]

Although reason demands that we announce to your brotherhood the beginnings of our episcopate, nevertheless, the favors of God . . . to be silent . . . .

Letter 10
Pope Hormisdas to Caesarius
11 September 515

Hormisdas came to power in Rome determined to put an end to the Acacian schism, which divided the churches of Rome and Constantinople for thirty-five years before it was ended in 519.[56] The schism arose in 484 when pope Felix (483–92) excommunicated Acacius, patriarch of Constantinople (471–89), because of his support for the *Henotikon*, a document composed by Acacius and issued by the emperor Zeno in 482 to reconcile the deep political and theological divisions that had arisen between supporters and opponents of the council of Chalcedon (451).[57] Negotiations to resolve the schism had languished during Symmachus's pontificate, but were resumed in 515 on the initiative of the emperor Anastasius.[58] Hormisdas sent a delegation to Constantinople under the leadership of Ennodius, bishop of Pavia, with instructions for negotiation. At the same time he decided to inform other western bishops of developments up to that point. It was in this context that he wrote the following letter to Caesarius and his suffragan bishops. That the letter also circulated outside Caesarius's province is clear from Avitus's comment that he received a copy in Vienne "from clerics of the church of Arles."[59]

---

[55] The Latin text is also available in note 1 to *Epist. Arel.* 29, ed. Gundlach, 42.

[56] *Liber pontificalis* 54, and Caspar (1930–3) II, 129–83.

[57] For a brief and lucid account of the theological issues in dispute, see Wilken (1990), 620–2. For a general narrative of events, see Beck (1980), 421–33.

[58] Richards (1979), 100–109.

[59] Avitus, *Epist.* 41.

HORMISDAS TO HIS MOST BELOVED BROTHER CAESARIUS AND TO THOSE UNDER THE AUTHORITY OF YOUR LOVE[60]

1. It is right that you who delight in the catholic communion rejoice with us at each and every opportunity for harmony in the church. Just as we share a single understanding of faith, so there should be an undivided rejoicing at good fortune. You know how the detestable heresy of Eutyches is creeping through the eastern churches,[61] and how many times the ecumenical council [of Chalcedon] has denounced the poison of this superstition, and how often the salutary warnings of the apostolic see have condemned its followers. Yet, as if ashamed to submit to the truth or to obey the preaching of the apostolic see, they nonetheless persist in their obstinacy. For pride always endangers salvation. It was because of pride that its discoverer, the devil, was deprived of angelic power. Along with us your brotherhood has often been distressed at these events, mindful of that instructive apostolic saying: "If one member suffers, all the members suffer together" [1 Cor. 12: 26]. But God, "who wants all people to be saved and to come to the knowledge of truth" [1 Tim. 2: 4], has now illuminated the senses of many people, and has given them a longing for apostolic communion. As a result, what they long preached in dissent, they now condemn in recantation. We have accepted their return without a hint of suspicion, because whoever confesses his sin without any pretense of an excuse shows a clear desire for amendment.

2. Therefore, in condemning their past error almost all the bishops of Dardania, Illyria, and Scythia seek communion with blessed Peter, chief of the apostles. By their letters and delegations they have agreed to obey the rulings of the apostolic see. Only [Christians] of fervent faith know how much we should rejoice for them. You should also be informed that they have now anathematized Nestorius as well, who divided the incarnation of our Lord Jesus Christ and through this tried to

---

[60] In Hormisdas' corpus the letter is *Epist.* 9, ed. Thiel, 758–61. It is also *Epist. Arel.* 30, ed. Gundlach, 43–4.

[61] Eutyches (*c*.378–454), the archimandrite of a monastery in Constantinople, maintained that Christ had a single nature. His beliefs were vindicated by the council of Ephesus in 449, but condemned by the council of Chalcedon in 451.

assert that there are two sons.[62] Eutyches has been condemned for the same reason. By not preaching that there are two natures in one person, he denied the reality of the flesh so as to implant into the churches of Christ, as he imagined, a Manichean idea. To these is added Dioscurus of Alexandria.[63] In agreeing with the aforementioned wickedness [of Eutyches], he shared his condemnation at the holy council of Chalcedon. Discovering the similar fruits that grow from evil seeds, he fell into the pit he prepared for the faithful. These heretics were succeeded by Timothy Aelurus[64] and Peter [Mongo],[65] whose iniquity matched theirs in every respect. They did not depart from their mendacious teachers in any way but surpassed them in every perversity. They were proven to be a source of general harm: their hands were stained by the flow of episcopal blood, and their ruin destroyed the lives of innocent people. They bear the marks of eternal damnation imprinted on them by catholics throughout the whole world. The orthodox have not only excommunicated them, they have also deprived them of the Christian name. Add to these [heretics] Peter [the Fuller] of Antioch[66] and his followers, as the other [orthodox Christians] I have mentioned have done. To be brief, suffice it to say only that Peter and his followers do not deviate in any way from the dogmas of those who have been condemned. When he formerly condemned these men, Acacius earned the praise of all Christians, and when he attacked those who laid claim to the Eutychian heresy, he appeared most pleasing to the faithful. But the devil hated him for defrauding him of his customary deceits. Afterwards, desiring to have these [heretics] as his own accomplices and turning his weapons against the catholics, Acacius suffered the same fate as those he wanted to have as partners.

---

[62] Nestorius, bishop of Constantinople (428–31), was deposed by the council of Ephesus in 431 for rejecting the title "mother of God" for the Virgin Mary. He denied the charge that he had taught that Jesus and Christ were two different persons.

[63] Dioscurus, bishop of Alexandria (444–51), had presided over the council of Ephesus in 449 as a supporter of Eutyches. He too was deposed by the council of Chalcedon.

[64] Monophysite bishop of Alexandria (457–60, 475–7).

[65] Monophysite bishop of Alexandria (477–90).

[66] Monophysite bishop of Antioch (470–1, 475–7, 482–8).

3. It would take too long to go through every detail in a brief letter. We have therefore sent a partial account of the entire matter for your information. For we believe that such an important matter cannot escape your notice, especially since our predecessors sent letters about it to your area. As for the events that have recently happened, we have taken care to instruct your brotherhood to prevent the wicked from being able to deceive the faithful because of their ignorance. As for those who strive to propagate such deceptions, they should be fully aware that they are banned from the fellowship of holy communion. Where faith is concerned, whatever pertains to the favor of this world should be rejected. Not even natural affection ought to be preferred to celestial concerns, so that we might fulfill that precept of the Lord: "Whoever loves father or mother more than me is not worthy of me" [Matt. 10: 37].

4. As for the other religious developments that we, trusting in divine beneficence, again await in the East at the present time, and about which we have sent envoys, petition the Lord Jesus Christ that he who granted a favorable beginning might by his goodness deign to grant a similar result. We have sent to your charity Urbanus, a *defensor* of the apostolic see, also suited for this business.[67] Through him we wish to learn by a fitting response your wishes for the disposition of all these issues. May God keep you safe, dearest brothers. Issued on September 11 in the consulship of the most distinguished Florentius [515].

Letter 11
Pope Felix IV to Caesarius
3 February 528

As *Letter* 19 demonstrates, Caesarius had considerable difficulty enforcing canon 2 of the council of Arles (524), which had required lay candidates for the higher clergy to live ascetically for a year before ordi-

---

[67] Urbanus is otherwise unknown. *Defensores* were agents of the bishop of Rome and other bishops who looked out for the church's legal interests. They played an important role in the administration of ecclesiastical property, especially the extensive holdings of the Roman church.

nation. He therefore asked pope Felix (526–30) for confirmation of the canon. Felix's response provided the support Caesarius had sought.

FELIX TO HIS MOST BELOVED BROTHER CAESARIUS[68]

I have read what your brother bishops decided, that no layman be abruptly promoted to episcopal office before undergoing a probationary period. You have also informed us that some have crossed back to the habits of secular life after ordination. Although such audacity is abominable, neglect is more dangerous. Someone who is capable of resisting an approaching evil and yet secretly permits it to occur, is himself instead revealed as the instigator of the evil deed. No one should expect to absolve himself by pointing to what was done in the past, for everything condemned for having had illicit beginnings cannot thereafter bear fruit. If something that is perfected in stages should arrive at its final stage before its instruction is complete, it will go astray at a time of examination, because it will not have become stable. Nor can anyone who has achieved success without hard work maintain his position by inducing fear. Empty praise injures the one who receives it, because it feeds his pride rather than calling him to the work of true virtue. [St. Paul], the "vessel of election," wrote to his house-slave Timothy and said: "You should not impose hands on anyone quickly, and you should not share in others' sins" [1 Tim. 5: 22]. Why does he say "you should not impose hands too quickly"? Because the office in question is conferred in such a way that it remains permanently. Before this happens, the matter should be deliberated at length. How can he be a schoolteacher who is ignorant of the ABCs? How can he be a ship captain who has not demonstrated his experience among sailors? He who has not bent his heart to obedience does not know what respect is owed to teachers; how is he to furnish his inferiors with an example of proper behavior in the house of God? Let all clerics, and particularly those who are to be chosen for the episcopate, take notice of this apostolic warning: "It is also necessary that he have a good reputation among outsiders" [1 Tim. 3: 7]. For this reason, choose a bishop to be ordained by common consensus and in observation of the venerable canons, so that we might take pains for our own salvation and take care of the needs of those who have been duly accepted into this rank. May

---

[68] The letter is *Epist. Arel.* 31, ed. Gundlach, 45.

God preserve you unharmed, dearest brother. Issued on February 3 [in the year] after the consulship of the most distinguished [Vettius Agorius Basilius] Mavortius [528].[69]

Letter 12
Pope John II to the bishops of Gaul
7 April 534

Caesarius convened the council of Marseille in May 533 to hear the case of bishop Contumeliosus of Riez, the senior suffragan in his diocese, who had been charged with illicit sexual relations (probably with his wife, to judge by the canons cited against him[70]) and unlawfully alienating houses belonging to his church, charges that were often politically motivated. Presented with the evidence against himself, Contumeliosus confessed and agreed to enter a monastery to undergo penance and to pay the church back for the property he had sold. The council was divided, however, on the length of time Contumeliosus should be suspended from office. Some of his colleagues believed he should be suspended from his position only while he performed his penance. Others, including Caesarius, maintained that he should be permanently deposed from office. Since all efforts to agree on this point failed, the council left unresolved both the duration of Contumeliosus' penance and the question of his continuation in office. It was to resolve these issues that Caesarius wrote to pope John at some point between May 533 and April 534. The pope responded with three letters; each upheld Caesarius's position and issued directions to a different party in the case. The first letter was addressed to the bishops of Gaul, principally in the province of Arles.

[69] In the West, dating by the post-consulship of the previous consul rather than the consulship of the current consul occurred when the name of the current western consul was unknown or when no western consul had been named for the year. The latter was the case in 528, when the emperor Justinian was the sole consul.
[70] If married at the time of their ordination, deacons, priests, and bishops in Gaul were required to refrain from further marital relations, Orange (441), can. 22, and Tours (461), can. 1, *CCSL* 148 (1963), 84, 143–4. See further the collection of canons known as II Arles (442/506), can. 2 and 3, *CCSL* 148 (1963), 114; and Gregory of Tours, *In gloria confessorum* 77, and *Hist.* I. 44. See also Brennan (1985).

JOHN TO HIS MOST BELOVED BROTHERS, ALL THE BISHOPS SERVING IN GAUL[71]

We have received the report your brotherhood sent in which Contumeliosus is said to have been implicated in many crimes. And because a person of this sort cannot be engaged in the sacred mysteries, our authority decrees that he be removed from his rank and office and be placed in a monastery, so that he may endeavor to ask the Lord's pardon for his fault. Nothing is impossible for his clemency, who can undo everything that has been done. But so that Contumeliosus' church is not deprived of leadership, we decree that a visitor be supplied to take his place. The visitor should realize that he is to administer everything in such a way that he makes no changes in the ranks of the clergy or church property, but only pursues those activities that pertain to the sacred mysteries. So that Contumeliosus might have the opportunity for repentance, however, we decree that he give you a sworn and dated declaration in which he publicly confesses his error. May God keep you safe, dearest brothers. Issued on April 7 during the consulship of the most distinguished Flavius Paulinus Junior [534].[72]

Letter 13
Pope John to the clergy of the church of Riez
6 April 534

In his letter to the clerics of the diocese of Riez John concerned himself with the authority of the visitor Caesarius was to appoint.

JOHN TO THE PRIESTS, DEACONS, AND CLERGY OF THE CHURCH IN WHICH CONTUMELIOSUS WAS BISHOP[73]

A report sent to us by our brothers and fellow bishops has arrived, in which Contumeliosus is said to have confessed to and been convicted

---

[71] The letter is *Epist. Arel.* 32, ed. Gundlach, 46.
[72] The title *Junior* was used in consular formulas to distinguish a later consul from an earlier one with the same name, in this case the consul of 534 from the consul of 498, Bagnall et al. (1987), 40–6.
[73] According to J. Sirmond (*PL* 66: 23, note a), the *codex Lirinensis* contained in addition the heading "Precept of pope John to the priests, deacons, and whole clergy of the church of Riez." The letter is *Epist. Arel.* 33.

of his crimes. And because he who is involved in misdeeds of this kind cannot perform the ministry of a bishop any longer, we have decided that it is necessary to provide you with the services of a visitor. And so our authority has decreed that a visitor be presented to his church, so that a church deprived of its own primate will not lack a bishop's services. We decree, however, that in all respects you should obey this visitor only in those matters that pertain to the sacred mysteries. That is, he should not presume to have anything to do with church property, nor should the clergy established in their present ranks be promoted to higher rank until the church acquires its own bishop. We have turned over all supervision of this matter to our brother and fellow bishop Caesarius, and we decree that he should take care of all necessary details. May God keep you safe, most beloved sons. Issued on April 6 during the consulship of the most distinguished Flavius Paulinus Junior [534].

Letter 14a
Pope John to Caesarius
April 534

In his third letter pope John spelled out Caesarius's responsibilities and reinforced them with a selection of canonical precedents.

JOHN TO HIS MOST BELOVED BROTHER CAESARIUS[74]

We were happy to receive the letter of your charity in which, besides mentioning material needs, you also made known what Contumeliosus has done. We feel pain at the loss of a bishop, but it is necessary to maintain the force of the canons. And so by our authority we have suspended Contumeliosus from episcopal office. For it is not right that someone polluted by sins should perform sacred duties. Under your supervision he should be sent to a monastery where, mindful of his sins, he should endeavor to pour out tears of repentance in order to win compassion from our Lord Jesus Christ, who has mercy on all men. Designate a visitor in his place until the church, which has been deprived of its bishop, can obtain its own. We for our part ought to beseech God in our common prayers that a bishop excel all the pure.

[74] The letter is *Epist. Arel.* 34, ed. Gundlach, 47–8.

But if any bishops happen to commit crimes in disregard of their rank, reveal their identity to everyone. For they will be more likely to be on their guard against wrongdoing, if they see that what they have done is not hidden from people. We have appended below what the canons require in these cases, so that you can learn what must be done. May God keep you safe, dearest brother.

These are the titles of the canons that my holy lord pope John sent to me with the authority of the apostolic see

1. The letter of holy Siricius, pope of Rome, to Himerius, bishop of Tarragona, among other matters, at a passage from chapter 7:[75]

"And because some of those we are speaking about, as your holiness has related, lament that it was because of ignorance that they lapsed"—that is, that they returned to their wives—"we rule that they should be treated mercifully. But this is on the condition that they remain for the rest of their lives in the same office they held when their sins were revealed, without any promotion, provided that after this they conscientiously demonstrate their self-control. As for those who rely on the excuse of illicit privilege, asserting that this [privilege] was granted them under the old law, let them know that they have been deposed by the authority of the apostolic see from every ecclesiastical office for which they appear unworthy. They will never be permitted to perform the venerable mysteries of which they deprived themselves when they became involved in obscene desires. And because the present examples forewarn us to be wary in the future, any bishop, priest, or deacon who has hereafter been discovered to be [a sinner] of this kind— which we hope does not happen—should know that we have now closed off to them every possibility of indulgence. For it is necessary that wounds that do not respond to the medicine of hot compresses be cut out by the knife."

---

[75] Siricius, *Epist.* 1. vii. 11, *PL* 13: 1140–1. Issued in 385, this is the first of the papal decretals. It was written in response to questions posed to Siricius's predecessor Damasus, and intended to carry the stamp of papal authority. See Caspar (1930–3) I, 261–2.

2. The Canons of the Apostles, can. 25.[76] That if a bishop, priest or deacon has been condemned for crimes, he should not be deprived of communion:

"A bishop, priest or deacon who has been caught in fornication or perjury should be deposed but not deprived of communion. For scripture says, 'The Lord will not punish him twice for it' [cf. Nahum 1: 9]."

3. The Canons of the Apostles, can. 29.[77] That those condemned of crimes should not regain possession of their former office:

"If any bishop, priest, or deacon has been justly deposed for proven sins, and dares to resume the ministry once entrusted to him, he should be completely cut off from the church."

4. The council of Neocaesarea [314/9], can. 95.[78] Concerning priests who have committed fornication:

"If a priest commits fornication or adultery, he ought furthermore to be deposed and required to do penance."

5. The council of Antioch [341], can. 4.[79] Concerning those who have been convicted and are trying to continue in their ministry:

"If any bishop convicted by a synod, or any priest or deacon convicted by his bishop dares to have anything to do with the holy ministry, whether as a bishop according to his prior rank or as a priest or deacon, he should not be permitted, not even in another council, to have any hope of restoration or chance to make amends. In addition, all those who communicate with him should be ejected from the church,

---

[76] Ed. F. X. Funk, *Didascalia et Constitutiones Apostolorum*, I (Paderborn, 1905), 571. This collection of eighty-five canons was composed in Greek in the late fourth century and later translated into Latin. Believed to be apostolic, it acquired a substantial influence over Greek and Latin canon law.
[77] Ibid., 573 (can. 28).
[78] Can. 1, ed. P.-P. Joannou, *Fonti*, fasc. IX, *Discipline générale antique (IVe–IXe s.)*, I. 2, *Les canons des Synodes Particuliers* (Rome, 1962), 75.
[79] Ibid., 107–8.

especially if they try to communicate with these men after they have learned that a verdict has been pronounced against them."

6. The council of Antioch [341], can. 15.[80] Concerning bishops unanimously deposed by bishops of the same province:

"If a bishop accused of proven sins is convicted by all the bishops of the same province, and all of them unanimously pass the same form of judgment against him, then he should not be judged by others, but the sentence of the bishops of his province who have agreed together should remain firm."

[Here] end the titles of the canons sent by holy pope John

Letter 14b
Caesarius to the bishops of Gaul
April 534

In an addendum to pope John's letter, aimed mainly at his suffragan bishops, Caesarius included a further list of precedents and his own commentary on the case. In the final paragraph he issued two regulations on Christian burial quite unrelated to the rest of the letter.

THE TITLES THAT FOLLOW ON THIS MATTER HAVE BEEN EXCERPTED FROM THE CANONS SO THAT EVERYONE MIGHT QUICKLY BE ABLE TO LEARN THAT CLERICS CANNOT BE RECALLED TO THEIR ORIGINAL POSITION AFTER [COMMITTING] MORTAL SINS[81]

At a passage from the council of Nicaea [325], that is, the council of 318 bishops:[82]

"If any happen to have been injudiciously promoted to the episcopate after they have confessed to a sin or been convicted of one by others, let them be removed."

---

[80] Ibid., 116
[81] These canons and the accompanying commentary are *Epist. Arel.* 35, ed. Gundlach, 49–54.
[82] A paraphrase of canon 2, *Decrees of the Ecumenical Councils*, ed. Tanner, 6–7.

[Here] begin the Gallic titles of the canons

1. The council of Valence, attended by 18 bishops, held July 12 during the third consulship of [the emperor] Gratian [that he shared] with Equitius [374]:[83]

"Brothers, we have decided to record something that is in accord with the interests of the church, so that you might know that if after ordination any deacon, priest, or bishop confesses himself to be polluted by a mortal sin, he should be removed from office, for he is guilty whether he confesses that this is true or falsely maintains that it is untrue. For what is punished when said of others cannot be absolved by those [clerics] who have confessed the same of themselves, since everyone who has become a cause of death for himself is a murderer. May divine piety protect you forever, most beloved brothers."

2. Likewise, at a passage from the council of Orléans [511], composed of 30 bishops:[84]

"If a deacon or priest commits a mortal sin, he should be deprived of his office and communion at the same time."

3. Likewise, at a passage from the council [held] in the church of Justus:[85]

"If after ordination into the clergy any deacon or priest is discovered to be having relations with his wife, let him be thrown out of office."

4. Likewise from the council of Epaone [517], composed of 34 bishops:[86]

"If any deacon or priest commits a mortal sin, let him be deposed from his office and exiled to a monastery. There only, for as long as he lives, should he be admitted to communion."

---

[83] Valence (374), can. 4, *CCSL* 148 (1963), 40.
[84] Orléans (511), can. 9, *CCSL* 148A (1963), 7.
[85] Orange (441), can. 22, *CCSL* 148 (1963), 84. I follow Février (1986b), 98, in identifying the *ecclesia Iustinianensis* (*ecclesia Iustianus* in some MSS) with Justus, who served as bishop of Orange at the time of the council.
[86] Epaone (517), can. 22, *CCSL* 148A (1963), 29–30.

1. It is very clearly established, according to what the canons of the ancient fathers as transmitted by the holy pope John, the opinion of the 318 bishops [at the council of Nicaea],[87] and the Gallic canons appear to maintain, that clerics who have been caught in adultery and have either confessed or been convicted by others cannot return to their office. Perhaps there will be people who because of misguided piety are not pleased by the severity of the holy fathers, as expressed above. If so, they should realize that they reprove and condemn the precepts of 318 bishops, the authority of the holy pope, and the opinions of those bishops who established the remaining canons under guidelines set by those 318 bishops. But perhaps they are more pious than the 318 bishops mentioned above, more merciful than the holy apostolic pope John, and more charitable than the rest of those holy bishops who decided this in their resolutions for the example and remedy of the churches. Let them therefore either obediently agree with the precepts of the bishops, or if not, let them realize that they are the opponents and enemies of all of them.

What kind of kindness is it—a kindness inimical to justice—to coddle wrong-doers and leave their wounds uncured until Judgment Day? But even if we were to see them performing the most rigorous penitence for many years, we would still have to counsel them about their salvation and so preserve the regulations of the canons. But some of these offenders never display the humility of compunction nor the perseverance of prayer and lamentation; nor do they imitate the blessed David, who said: "I shall wash my bed every night; I shall moisten my bedding with tears" [Ps. 6: 6] and: "I used to eat ashes just like bread, and I used to mix my drink with weeping" [Ps. 102: 9]; nor do we see them make time for fasting and reading. In such cases, if they were to return to their former rank, we can predict the degree of negligence, tepidity, and spiritually harmful security in which they would remain. For they would believe that God had pardoned them, despite their unworthy repentance, in the same way as their fellow bishops would appear to have pardoned them.

---

[87] Caesarius repeatedly stresses the affirmation of the canons of Nicaea by 318 bishops. The significance of the number may depend on Abraham's 318 servants in Gen. 14: 14, Arnold (1894), 381.

Truly I say that when those we seem to have pardoned with dangerous and false mercy come before the tribunal of Christ to be condemned
for such great sins, they will take the stand against us. They will
charge that while we feared their harsh criticism or gladly accepted their
false flattery and dangerous adulation and thus pardoned them to no good
purpose, we permitted them to remain in sin or even to increase their
sins, and we did not remember what was written in the Old Testament,
that when one man sinned, God's anger raged furiously against all. O
piety, O mercy, to spare one and lead all into judgment by bad example!
The holy and most blessed martyr Cyprian does not urge us to act thus
when he says, "Whoever coddles the sinner with adoring words supplies
fuel for sin. He does not check his faults but fosters them." He also
wrote, "The physician who treats the swelling surfaces of wounds with
a timid hand and allows the poison hidden in deep recesses to increase
while he watches is incompetent."[88] St. John [Chrysostom], bishop of
Constantinople, argued the same: "Unskilled is the physician who puts
a scar on the wound before he has eliminated the infection."[89]

And so consider carefully whether it can or ought to happen that by
despising the canons of so many and such great bishops whom we have
mentioned above, we should presume to think or act contrary to their
precepts. [And keep in mind] in particular that if we neglect the holy
decrees of those 318 bishops who ordered councils to take place in all
churches, we do not despise them alone, but as I already said above, we
sinfully despise in our souls the bishops from Africa and elsewhere who
have passed legislation in matters of ecclesiastical discipline under the
guidelines these bishops set down for the whole world. I do not dare at
all to take this risk myself, because my merits are not so great that I
can presume to take personal responsibility for the sins of others. Nor
do I have so much eloquence that I can plead my case before the tribunal
of Christ against such great and such holy bishops who laid down the
canons. Everyone who decides to feel or think differently should consider how he can give an account on Judgment Day. Insofar as God
deigns to give me strength, I wish to obey their precepts conscientiously, because I do not desire to quarrel with them, but to be at peace

---

[88] Cyprian, *De lapsis* 14, ed. G. Hartel, *CSEL* 3. 1 (1868), 247. Caesarius
quotes from the same passage of Cyprian in *Serm.* 148. 1.
[89] The source of this quotation is unknown.

with them and to have some sort of alliance with them. And so we must take diligent care that if, as has been written above, there are clerics who return to their wives, they are to be completely suspended from office. And if there are also men twice married or the husbands of women married twice, although they certainly do no wrong, they cannot be ordained as clerics; if they have been ordained, they are to be deposed.[90] Lord Faustus [of Riez] wrote about them in a letter: "He who still wishes to behave as a husband has lost the grace of a consecrated man."[91] Since this is the case, in what sense can anyone say that someone who has committed adultery can return to his office?

Someone may say at this juncture, "You therefore deny the mercy of God, who said, 'I do not want the sinner to die, but to be converted and live' [Ezek. 33: 11], and 'Will the man who falls not try to rise up again?' [Ps. 41: 8; Isa. 24: 20], and 'On the day a sinner is converted, all his iniquities are consigned to oblivion' [Ezek. 18: 21–2]." We can and must respond frankly to this objection; far be it from us to appear to doubt these sayings even slightly. For we most certainly believe that whoever does penance worthily until the end of his life will not only receive pardon but also eternal rewards. On account of ecclesiastical law, however, and out of respect for the statutes of the ancient fathers—which far be it from us to dare to criticize or transgress!—we know by the precepts of the fathers that such a man ought not to be returned to clerical office, even though we believe that he will obtain eternal life after a well-performed penance. This is so [well-established a principle] that it is written in the canons: "No penitent should ever be ordained a cleric."[92] If the man who seeks penance on his own cannot be ordained as a bishop or a priest, even if he performs his penance perfectly (with the result that even if a man has been ordained in ignorance and is later proven to have done penance, he is deposed from office), then why is a man sent against his will to a monastery to do penance—should he be described as anything other than a "penitent"?—permitted to return to episcopal office?

---

[90] Agde (506), can. 1, *CCSL* 148 (1963), 193; Arles (524), can. 3, *CCSL* 148A (1963), 44.

[91] This document does not survive; see Engelbrecht's comments in *CSEL* 21 (1891), 220.

[92] Agde (506), can. 43, *CCSL* 148 (1963), 211.

Let no one offer me any other objections against the authority of the apostolic see, the precepts of 318 bishops, or the rules of the other canons, because I do not doubt that it is not only audacious but even dangerous to agree with objections raised against the definition of those bishops in whom the Holy Spirit has spoken. For I deeply fear and tremble at the condemnation that the priest Eli deservedly received on account of his foolish indulgence [cf. 1 Sam. 1–4].[93] Because he negligently chastised his sons, wishing neither to beat nor to banish them, they were killed within a single day, 30,000 people were slain, and the ark of the covenant was captured. Eli died of a broken neck after falling backward and his name was eliminated from the book of life. Phinehas, on the other hand, because he killed two adulterers together when moved by the zeal of God, liberated the whole people from God's anger [cf. Num. 25].

I do not adduce this example to suggest that the bishops of the Lord ought to take revenge now by putting people to death, as he did, but rather to suggest that it is better that each person bear shame and confusion in the short time that he lives in this world, than that he later experience eternal punishment. And it is much more useful as an example to others for him to be removed from office, to do penance for as long as he lives, and to find healing for himself on the day of need. As for anyone who wishes to oppose my humble self in this case, I do not intend to give him any other response than what the aforementioned canons contain. I therefore state that while those committing mortal sins are soon forgiven, many who fear neither God nor the judgments of ecclesiastical discipline deceive themselves and induce people of another religion to defame the reputation of the Christian faith when they shamelessly and impiously take illicit familiarities with other women. It is therefore just to impose a proper end to this grave evil by closing off the possibility of returning to office, as all the canons demand.

Yet some clerics lapse into a sin, especially adultery, by the devil's persuasion and in complete disregard for their souls; when they subsequently take notice of canonical rules, they try as hard as they can, by putting on the appearance of piety, not to be sent into monasteries. If

---

[93] See Caesarius, *Serm.* 5. 1.

they are sent there, they try after a brief time to return to office by coercion, with an insolence that is both excessive and hostile to ecclesiastical discipline. Whoever does not reject this document with the titles of the canons written above and does not despise it for its rustic language, will be able to receive much help from it against the enemies of ecclesiastical law, so that he might freely say, as was already said above, that he can in no way oppose such sacred rulings of the ancient fathers. In saying this with all humility I absolve my conscience in God's eyes. But whoever is disposed by insolence, adulation, or false flattery not to uphold the severity of ecclesiastical discipline, let him consider how he will excuse himself before Christ's tribunal, where all those who laid down the regulations will not hesitate to take the stand against him. As for those lord bishops of mine who receive this document, if they not only do [not] offer it to other bishops to read but also do not wish to have it transcribed, let them fear having to render an account on Judgment Day.

2. We believe that we should also rule in the matter of those who have been put to death for their crimes by governors or by rulers of the people, and have been buried in Christian cemeteries. We decree in accordance with canonical regulations[94] that permission to offer gifts [on behalf of their souls] is not to be denied. As for the violators of tombs, although the law of the emperors condemns them to death,[95] nevertheless, if any survive after being caught in this crime, they are to be deprived of ecclesiastical communion, for it is wrong not to deny the fellowship of Christians to those who rashly dare to disquiet the remains of the dead.

[94] Orléans (533), can. 15, *CCSL* 148A (1963), 101.
[95] Valentinian III, *Nov.* 23 (447), ed. T. Mommsen and P. M. Meyer, 114–7. This law was also valid in post-Roman Gaul, having been incorporated into the Visigothic lawcode, *Breviarium Alarici*, Valentinian, *Nov.* 5, ed. G. Haenel, *Lex Romana Visigothorum* (Leipzig, 1849, repr. Aalen, 1962), 280.

Letter 15
Pope Agapitus to Caesarius
18 July 535

In May 535 the archdeacon Agapitus was elected to succeed pope John. When Caesarius asked his permission to alienate some church property, Agapitus acted to uphold the law originally passed by the council of Rome (502) under Symmachus, which sharply restricted the practice. In view of the fact that he had attended the council as one of Symmachus's deacons, this was not a surprising response. It is unclear what property was involved here. Pointing to the probable involvement of the papal *defensor* Emeritus in the case, whose duty was the protection of papal property (see *Letter* 16), and also to the pope's explanation that he was not denying the request because of parsimony, Caspar plausibly suggested that the property Caesarius wanted to alienate belonged to the patrimony of Rome in Arles.[96] It is also possible, however, that it belonged to the church of Arles, as in *Letters* 7a and 18. There is less uncertainty about the beneficiaries of the proposed transfer of property. According to Agapitus, they were the "poor," in all likelihood the sisters of Caesarius's monastery.

AGAPITUS TO HIS MOST BELOVED BROTHER CAESARIUS[97]

Because of our deep commitment, by God's grace, to give most generously to the poor the support they need and because of our affection for your brotherhood, we in no way consider it burdensome for us to grant what you request. But the venerable and very clear regulations of the fathers prevent us from doing so, for they specifically prohibit us from transferring to the ownership of others by whatever title the properties owned by the church, over which the almighty Lord has put us in charge. We believe that your wisdom too approves of the view that we not presume on any pretext or out of deference to any individual to violate laws and rules decreed long ago. Do not think that we do this because we are parsimonious or seek worldly profit. But in view of divine judgment it is necessary for us to maintain inviolately everything decreed by the holy authority of councils. To make this clear to your

---

[96] Caspar (1930–3) II, 205.
[97] The letter is *Epist. Arel.* 36, ed. Gundlach, 55.

charity beyond question, we have had extracted specific passages pertain-
ing to this issue from the regulations of the fathers, which we believed
should be sent to you along with these comments. May God keep you
safe, dearest brother. Issued July 18 [in the year] after the consulship of
the most distinguished Paulinus Junior [535].

From the decision of the council, among other matters and at the
[relevant] passage:[98]

"After considering these matters, therefore, we decree by a decision
that will remain in force by the aid of our God that no one from this
day forward, for as long as the saving doctrine of the catholic faith shall
abide, the Lord willing, should be permitted to transfer to anyone's
ownership, under any form of alienation, a rural estate of any size,
however large or small. No exemptions based on any pretext of necessity should be granted, since what we are saying is not personal [but
general in its application]. Nor should any cleric or layman be protected on the strength of such a pretext."

And a little further:[99]

"We wish the priests of Rome to be bound by the religious obligations of this decree. Anyone who is so forgetful of God and oblivious
of this decree as to try to violate it by alienating anything should be
punished by the loss of his office. In addition, anyone who seeks or accepts [land alienated in this way], or any priest, deacon, or *defensor* who
supports anyone who gives up [such land] should be penalized by the
anathema by which souls are stricken by an angry God. As for the
people mentioned above, that is, the people whom we decreed to be
anathematized, let the prescribed penalty that we have directed against
the donor be preserved and inflicted on the one who receives [the land]
and on the one who subscribes [to the transaction], unless perhaps the
donor also looks out for his own welfare by swiftly demanding back
[what he has given away]. But if anyone out of a lack of concern for
his own soul perhaps neglects the remedy we have offered, then in addition to the penalties mentioned above, if any written agreement has
been drawn up illegally, it is completely invalidated, however much it

[98] Ed. T. Mommsen, *MGH AA* 12 (1894), 449.
[99] Ibid., 450.

was invalid from the beginning. In addition, all clerics are permitted to bring actions to contest [such transactions] and to be supported by ecclesiastical authority, so that [the church] can demand back donations and their profits, and so that he who wrongly and impiously disperses gifts left by religious people for the maintenance of the poor might have nothing with which to protect himself before Christ's tribunal."

Letter 16
Pope Agapitus to Caesarius
18 July 535

Within a short time after he had been sent into exile by the council of Marseille (*Letters* 12–14), Contumeliosus had moved back to Riez, resumed his episcopal see, and appealed his case to the bishop of Rome. Mistakenly informed by his *defensor* that Caesarius had agreed to this sequence of events, Agapitus agreed to consider Contumeliosus' appeal. On the same day that he wrote *Letter* 15 to Caesarius, Agapitus wrote the following letter, informing him of his decision.

AGAPITUS TO HIS MOST BELOVED BROTHER CAESARIUS[100]

We had hoped, most beloved brother, that bishop Contumeliosus' reputation would have remained blameless, and that there would have been neither any need for your judgment in the past nor any reason for us to pass judgment now. This is especially so because reverence for our common office somehow seems to have suffered an attack in the accusation of this man. For this reason, since he confidently asserts his innocence and wishes to seek the assistance of an appeal, let us constantly pray that the benefit of a second trial might absolve him and restore him to universal favor. With the assistance of our God we shall therefore commission an inquiry to investigate, according to the regulations of the venerable canons and with the utmost diligence and concern for justice, every accusation that was considered under your supervision in this case. For it is not fitting for this man to be weighed down by the results of the previous inquiry, since he himself has sought a new judgment. For as we read, "The affection of the heart should not be

---

[100] The letter is *Epist. Arel.* 37, ed. Gundlach, 56–7.

turned away from the prayers of the sick when they are in need" [Tobit 4: 7]. May the Lord prevent the possibility of the words of Proverbs being said to us, "He who closes his ears so as not to hear a sick man will also call on God, and there will be no one to hear him" [Prov. 21: 13]. Who is more sick than bishop Contumeliosus, who in a time of tribulation is both upset by the shame of the previous judgment and disturbed by the anticipation of the coming inquiry? However much the purity of innocence may favor him—something which is to be hoped for—he cannot avoid anxiety about the outcome of the inquiry. Although the *defensor* Emeritus reported that Contumeliosus went back to his church by permission of your charity—we have rebuked him for this false statement—we nonetheless want the bishop, having recently recovered his own property, to be suspended from the management of the ecclesiastical patrimony and the celebration of Mass until the conclusion of the inquiry we have commissioned. For if the truth supports him, he will receive what was apparently taken away from him in the [first] inquiry more gloriously [if he awaits the second] inquiry than if he takes it by force. After he requested an inquiry by appealing to the apostolic see, however, your brotherhood would have done better if you had permitted none of his personal privileges to be reduced from the time of the judgment, so that the privileges he sought to resolve by the appeal would remain intact. For if the first judgment is put into effect, the second inquiry cannot grant what he might seek [to regain].[101] Add the fact that even if bishop Contumeliosus had not contested the judgment, he could according to the canons have sought a private withdrawal [from the city] rather than receive the severity of official banishment. Therefore, with bishop Contumeliosus suspended, as we said, only from that function which he is said to have usurped, namely, the celebration of Mass, and with the patrimony of the church placed in the control of his church's archdeacon, in such a manner that the bishop is provided with sufficient financial support, we order you to designate a visitor in his place and patiently await the judges we choose by the Lord's inspiration to hear the case. In addition, so that nothing might seem unfamiliar to your charity, we have with zealous love had attached

---

[101] Agapitus here appears to differentiate between Contumeliosus' official duties, which he could regain by vindication in a second trial, and his personal privileges (such as his loss of freedom and personal property), which an acquittal could not return to him.

chapters of the relevant constitutions below so that we might share in common knowledge of the canons, just as we share in affection.[102] May God keep you safe, dearest brother. Issued July 18 [during the year] after the consulship of the most distinguished Paulinus Junior [535].

Letter 17
Pope Vigilius to Caesarius
6 May 538

When the Franks took Provence in 536/7, most of Caesarius's ecclesiastical province fell under the control of king Childebert. Several dioceses, however, came under the jurisdiction of his nephew king Theodebert. It was probably therefore as metropolitan of the province of Arles rather than as papal vicar of Gaul that Caesarius was asked by pope Vigilius to intervene in a case of incestuous marriage that Theodebert had originally brought to the pope's attention. Why the king had consulted the pope about this case in the first place is uncertain. Violations of church laws governing the permissible degrees of marriage did not normally require papal intervention; that this case did suggests a serious disagreement at the local level, either between the king and the bishops or among the bishops themselves. That Theodebert would choose in the face of such a disagreement to consult the bishop of Rome rather than settle the question himself suggests a particular interest in aligning himself with the bishop of Rome, a policy consistent with his ambitions to regional supremacy.[103]

VIGILIUS TO HIS MOST BELOVED BROTHER CAESARIUS[104]

If in observing the commands of heaven it is fitting for every bishop to instruct the children of the catholic church, "welcome or unwelcome" [2 Tim. 4: 2], then it is far more necessary to respond appropriately to those who with a laudable piety seek advice about matters of which they are unsure. For this reason we have decided that it is necessary to consider the inquiry of our glorious son, king Theodebert,

---

[102] These are missing from the document.
[103] Collins (1983).
[104] This letter is *Epist. Arel.* 38, ed. Gundlach, 57–8.

which he communicated to us through his legate, the illustrious Moderic.[105] In his request his Majesty wishes to learn what form of penance can cleanse the sin of a man who illegally dared to marry his brother's wife.[106] Through a letter sent to the king, whose tenor your brotherhood will discover in the following comments, we took care to inform him that it would take no small measure of heartfelt repentance to expiate such a sin. But because, as we trust your charity well knows, the administration of penance is best entrusted to the supervision of local bishops, who can issue the remedy of a pardon in accordance with the degree of remorse, we believed it best to leave this matter to your judgment. For this reason, when your charity has considered the nature of the whole matter and the remorse of the penitent, you should be sure to inform our son the glorious king about the length of the penance and earnestly command him to prevent any such deed from being committed in the future. The man who has admitted this sin should take great care not to return "to the same vomit" [Prov. 26: 11], and he and his wife should live in separate accommodations. In this way they will both be rendered immune from every suspicion of the crime they committed. May God keep you safe, dearest brother. Issued May 6 during the consulship of the most distinguished Flavius Johannes [538].

Letter 18
Pope Hormisdas to Caesarius
514/23

At some point between 514 and 523 Caesarius wrote to Hormisdas with two requests for the nunnery, that it be given immunity from direct control by Caesarius's successors and that it be permitted to keep the proceeds made from the sale of church property. The first request was designed to ensure the monastery's independence after Caesarius's

---

[105] Moderic is otherwise unknown, *PLRE* IIIB, 894.
[106] This action was normally motivated by the desire of a man's kinsfolk to retain control over family property after his death. Such forms of incest were condemned for Theodebert's kingdom by the council of Clermont (535), can. 12, *CCSL* 148A (1963), 107–8.

death, and the second to help guarantee its security.[107] Hormisdas wrote back granting both of Caesarius's requests. His response was then signed by seven of Caesarius's suffragan bishops to strengthen its authority. Along with the *Testament, Life,* and *Rule for Nuns,* the letter became part of a dossier of documents designed to protect the monastery after Caesarius's death, a status underscored by its survival only as an appendix to the *Rule* in a ninth-century manuscript of the *Codex regularum* of Benedict of Aniane.

HORMISDAS TO HIS MOST BELOVED
BROTHER CAESARIUS[108]

1. I rejoice in the Lord, most beloved brother. I rejoice unceasingly that your zeal for religious faith is so strong that you keep tireless and careful watch to improve by new advances whatever pertains to the worship of God in his church. As for your other duties, you are not satisfied unless you are constantly adding something new. In your faith there is a special care and a firm resolve; you are like the prophet beloved by God who said, "I always hoped in you, Lord" [Ps. 71: 1], and then, not believing this devotion to be sufficient, added, "And I will add to all your praise" [Ps. 71: 14]. True love is not usually content with obedience, and charity thinks itself defective unless it burns with fervent devotion. Although God, who sees and knows secrets, observes faith deep in the heart, he does not permit his providence to be hidden or his treasury to be concealed without being increased. He orders his worshippers to bring their secret reverence into the open and to sing his praise with resounding exultation. I have said this because you indicated in your letter that you recently set up in the church of Arles, in addition to the customary troops of clerics and monks, choruses of women devoted to God. You requested that your successors not be permitted to have any power at any time in the women's monastery you recently established, so that the virgins consecrated to God might be free of all disturbance and annoyance and might freely be able to serve almighty God without interruption.

---

[107] See further Klingshirn (1990). On papal grants of immunity to monasteries, of which this is the first known example, see Ewig (1979), 414.
[108] This translation is based on de Vogüé's text of the letter in de Vogüé–Courreau, 352–8. The text is also available in Morin II, 125–7, and Thiel, 988–90.

2. It is an act of foresight worthy of a bishop's role to urge hearts to dedicate their chastity to God, and offer to his sacred worship the fruit of virginity from these mystic seeds. In the Scriptures the apostle declared this to be his greatest prayer: "I have betrothed you to one man, a chaste virgin to present to Christ" [2 Cor. 11: 2]. Therefore we most willingly approve the requests of your brotherhood, and affirm and decree by apostolic authority that none of your episcopal successors should ever dare to appropriate for himself any power in the monastery. The only exception is that in the pious exercise of pastoral responsibilities, the bishop and his clerics may visit the household of Christ the Lord that dwells there, provided they do so with sincere intentions and at convenient times, in keeping with what is fitting. It is therefore right that men and women established in suitable places should celebrate God's glory with equal devotion together, just as each waits with secure and complete faith for the hope of redemption.

3. You also request that we confirm by our authority a sale [of church property] and a donation that your love previously made on behalf of this monastery of women, with the additional hope that the alienation of ecclesiastical estates will not be allowed in the future, since it is prohibited by our decrees. We approve your proposal and admit your wish to be praiseworthy in that we rejoice that these same actions will also not be permitted to you in the future. But it is not proper to alienate what should rightly be granted from the resources of the church for the support of those who serve it. It is fitting that a good deed be performed without payment.[109] The reward of upright zeal ought to be hoped for rather than demanded, to prevent the remuneration of charity from being diminished through the advantage of a sale.[110] In regard to the monastery of virgins, we nonetheless confirm what you have sold and donated. At the same time we prohibit the alienation of ecclesiastical estates by this decree. Convey this to all the bishops

---

[109] For this sense of *fructus*, see *TLL* VI. 1, col. 1384, line 83 – col. 1385, line 6, and esp. Gal. 5: 22.

[110] This is a difficult passage. Hormisdas seems to suggest that the buyers of church property should simply have given their money to the monastery as a gift, rather than as payment for something in return (a sale). Otherwise, their remuneration for charity (in heaven) might be diminished. For a different interpretation, see de Vogüé–Courreau, 347–8.

belonging to the province under your supervision; for it is right that they all obey what is ordered for the common good. May God keep you safe, dearest brother.

I, bishop Marcellus [of Senez], have read and agreed to this.
I, John [of Fréjus], have agreed to and signed this.
I, Severus,[111] have agreed to and signed this.
I, Cyprianus [of Toulon], have read and agreed to this.
I, bishop Contumeliosus [of Riez], have read and agreed to this.
I, bishop Montanus,[112] have read and agreed to this.
I, Peter,[113] in the name of Christ, have read and agreed to this.

Letter 19
Caesarius et al. to bishop Agroecius of Antibes
6 November 527

One of the items on the agenda of the council of Carpentras (527) was the case of Agroecius, bishop of Antibes. He was accused of ordaining a cleric who had not undergone the year of probation required by the council of Arles (524), can. 2. Because Agroecius did not attend the council, Caesarius and his suffragans wrote this letter to inform him of their decision. Agroecius's reaction is not known.

BISHOP CAESARIUS AND THE OTHER BISHOPS GATHERED AT THE COUNCIL OF CARPENTRAS TO OUR HOLY LORD AND VENERABLE BROTHER BISHOP AGROECIUS[114]

You ought to have attended this council yourself or sent a representative, so that you might have given the synod an account of the ordination you are said to have performed. Then if you had performed it legally, you would have gone home charitably absolved by the favor of God. If on the other hand it had been established that you certainly transgressed the canons, you would have recognized by this announce-

---

[111] See unknown, represented at Arles (524).
[112] See unknown, present at Arles (524).
[113] See unknown.
[114] This letter is preserved with the canons of the council of Carpentras; its Latin text can be found in Morin II, 65–6, and in *CCSL* 148A (1963), 50–1.

ment that a decision promulgated by God's mediation may either strike down a defendant or absolve a suppliant. For although it is not right for bishops to be unaware of the canons, it would have been a less serious error if you had failed through ignorance than if you had transgressed canons that you or your representative had signed. As it is, however, you are guilty of a double fault, since you are proven to have recklessly sinned not only against the decrees of the venerable fathers but also against your own.[115]

Therefore, by our common deliberation in Christ we decree that because you violated the statutes [by ordaining][116] our son Protadius, you should suffer the penalty contained in the canons and should not presume to celebrate Mass for a year. For it is right that what was decided by bishops with God's mediation should be preserved inviolately by divine favor. What regard will our successors show for observing this law if it is first violated by those who established it?

I, bishop Caesarius, have signed.
I, bishop Cyprianus [of Toulon], have signed.
I, bishop Constantius [of Gap], have signed.
I, bishop Porcianus [of Digne], have signed.
I, bishop Gallicanus [of Embrun], have signed.
I, bishop Aletius [of Vaison], have signed.
I, bishop Heraclius [of Saint-Paul-Trois-Châteaux], have signed.
I, bishop Principius,[117] have signed.
I, bishop Contumeliosus [of Riez], have signed.
I, bishop Julianus [of Carpentras], have signed.
I, bishop Filagrius [of Cavaillon], have signed.
I, bishop Eucherius [of Avignon], have signed.
I, bishop Prosper [of Vence], have signed.
I, bishop Uranius,[118] have signed.
I, bishop Lupercianus [of Fréjus], have signed.
I, bishop Vindimialis [of Orange], have signed.

[115] Agroecius was represented at the council of Arles by the priest Catafronius, who signed in his place.
[116] Reading *ordinavisti*, Maassen.
[117] See unknown, also present at Orléans (511) and Orange (529) and represented at Vaison (529).
[118] See unknown.

Letter 20
Pope Boniface to Caesarius
25 January 531

Caesarius's most important theological achievement was the council of Orange (529), whose twenty-five canons steered a middle course between an extreme "Augustinian" emphasis on grace and predestination and an extreme "Pelagian" emphasis on free will.[119] Faced with continued opposition to his views after the council Caesarius wrote to pope Felix for support. Felix had died in September 530, however, and in a disputed election was succeeded by both Boniface, his own candidate, and Dioscurus, the clergy's candidate.[120] Even after Dioscurus's death in October 530, Boniface found it difficult to consolidate his authority. It was not therefore until January 531 that he found it possible to answer the letter Caesarius had written to Felix.

BONIFACE TO HIS MOST BELOVED BROTHER CAESARIUS[121]

1. We received your letter through our son the priest and abbot Arminius.[122] You sent it to us apparently still unaware of the episcopal office conferred upon us by the love that binds us to God. In your letter you thought it necessary to request our influence in obtaining what you had asked of our predecessor pope Felix of blessed memory to strengthen the Catholic faith. But because the divine will arranged matters in such a way that what you had hoped to obtain from him through us, you are now to obtain from us instead, we have not delayed granting a catholic response to your petition, which you formulated with the praiseworthy concern of faith. For you inform us that some Gallic bishops, although they admit that other good gifts originate from God's

[119] For the context, see *Life* I. 60. Excellent articles on "grace," "Pelagius," "Pelagianism," "predestination," and "prevenient grace" can be found with recent bibliography in the *Encyclopedia of Early Christianity*, ed. E. Ferguson (New York and London, 1990), *s.v.*
[120] *Liber pontificalis* 57.
[121] Morin published the Latin text of this letter with his text of the council of Orange, Morin II, 67–70. The text is also available in *CCSL* 148A (1963), 66–9. An English translation of the entire council, including Boniface's letter, is available in Burns (1981), 109–28.
[122] Arminius is otherwise unknown.

grace, assert that our faith in Christ is from nature rather than grace. They maintain—impious statement—that from the time of Adam faith for mankind has been a matter of free will, and that not even now is it conferred on individuals by the bounty of divine mercy. You request that in order to remove ambiguity we confirm by the authority of the apostolic see your creed in which you confess that on the contrary true faith in Christ and the beginning of all good will, according to catholic truth, is inspired into the limited senses of individuals by the intervention of God's grace.[123]

2. Many fathers and above all bishop Augustine of blessed memory, as well as our predecessors in the apostolic see, have discussed this matter so extensively that no one should doubt any more that faith indeed comes to us from grace. Therefore, we have decided to forgo an involved response. This is especially the case since—according to those opinions you have cited from the apostle in which he said: "I pursued mercy so that I might be faithful" [1 Cor. 7: 25], and "To you it is given on behalf of Christ not only to believe in him but also to suffer for his sake" [Phil. 1: 29]—it appears obvious that our faith in Christ, like all good things, comes to individuals from the gift of divine grace and not from the power of human nature. We rejoice that your brotherhood perceived this truth in accordance with catholic faith, when a council of some of the bishops of Gaul was held. As you have indicated, they decided unanimously that our faith in Christ is conferred on men by the intervention of divine grace. They added that there is absolutely nothing good in God's eyes that anyone can wish, begin, do, or complete without the grace of God, for as our Savior said, "Without me you can do nothing" [John 15: 5]. For it is both a certainty and an article of catholic faith that in all good things, the greatest of which is faith, divine mercy intervenes for us when we are not yet willing [to believe], so that we might become willing; it remains in us when we are willing [to believe]; and it follows us so that we remain in faith. As David the prophet says: "My God will intervene for me in his mercy" [Ps. 59: 10], and again: "My mercy is with him" [Ps. 89: 24], and elsewhere: "His mercy will follow me" [Ps. 23: 6]. Likewise, the blessed Paul says, "Who has given him something first and will be

[123] For this translation of *per praevenientem dei gratiam*, see Burns (1981), 110.

repaid for it? For all things are from him and through him and in him" [Rom. 11: 35–6]. For this reason we are very much surprised that those who believe the opposite are still so weighed down with the residue of an ancient error that they believe that people come to Christ not by a gift of God but by a gift of nature. Moreover, they say that the goodness of nature itself, which is known to have been perverted by Adam's sin, is the source of our faith rather than Christ. They do not realize that they are contradicting the Lord's saying: "No one comes to me unless it has been granted to him by my Father" [John 6: 44], and are opposing the blessed Paul crying out to the Hebrews: "Let us run in the contest set before us, gazing at Jesus Christ who originates and perfects our faith" [Heb. 12: 1–2]. Since this is the case, we cannot discover why they assign belief in Christ to the human will without the grace of God, when Christ originates and perfects our faith. For this reason, congratulating you with all due regard, we affirm that the statement of your faith written above conforms to the catholic regulations of the fathers.

3. As for those who, as you indicated in your report, wish to attribute other goods to grace and put faith in second place, we are compelling them by their own belief to be increasingly forced to ascribe faith to the gift of grace, apart from which there is nothing good that anyone can perform in God's eyes. As the blessed apostle says, "Everything that is not from faith is sin" [Rom. 14: 23]. Since this is the case, either they will attribute no good to grace, if they try to take faith away from it, or if they say that anything good comes from grace, they will necessarily have to attribute faith itself to grace. For if there is nothing good without faith, and if it is denied that faith itself comes from grace, then no good should be attributed to grace, which is impossible. For the apostle James says, "Every good gift and every perfect gift is from above, descending from the father of lights" [Jas. 1: 17]. But even these people admit, as you say, that other gifts are given through grace; they do not doubt that all these good gifts subsist by faith. Therefore, faith will necessarily be attributed to grace, from which they cannot separate the good that they attribute to grace.

4. Having therefore briefly discussed these matters, we decided there must be no response to the remaining inanities of Pelagian error

apparently contained in the letter that you reported was sent to you by a certain bishop. For we hope that divine mercy will deign through the ministry and teaching of your brotherhood to work so well in the hearts of all those you have reported as dissenters that they might believe from this that all good will comes not from themselves but from divine grace, and that they may find themselves now wishing to defend what they persistently struggled to attack. For it has been written: "The will is prepared by the Lord" [Prov. 8: 35, Septuagint], and elsewhere: "I know that I cannot be continent unless God grants it, and this itself was the mark of wisdom, to know whose gift it was" [Wisd. 8: 21]. May God keep you safe, dearest brother. Issued January 25 during [the year following] the consulship of the most distinguished Lampadius and Orestes [531].[124]

Letter 21
Caesarius to Caesaria the Elder
506/8

Like his *Testament* and *Letter* 18, this letter testifies to Caesarius's particular interest in the monastic lives of women. Addressed to his sister Caesaria in her capacity as head of a community of ascetic women, it draws on a long patristic heritage of advice to widows and virgins in order to warn of the dangers of male-female relationships, provide practical rules for the maintenance of chastity, and encourage the giving of alms to the poor.[125] It was almost certainly written before the dedication in 512 of the monastery of St. John in Arles (*Life* I. 35) and the nearly simultaneous promulgation of the *Rule for Nuns* (*Regula virginum* 48). For despite its obsession with the threat to chastity posed by excessive "familiarity" with outsiders, the letter makes no mention of the elaborate cloister regulations that characterized

[124] Because Boniface did not become bishop of Rome until 22 September 530, the text must be emended to indicate the post-consulship (531) rather than the consulship (530) of Lampadius and Orestes. The unusual naming of both consuls in the dating formula can be attributed to the fact that both men were westerners, Bagnall et al. (1987), 595.
[125] On the interrelation of these subjects with one another and with the larger themes implied by ascetic sexual renunciation, see Brown (1988), esp. 259–84 and 366–86.

the monastery and its early rule.[126] It may be possible to date the letter even earlier if we assume that Caesarius would not have used a metaphor of the integrity of the church plate (*Letter* 21. 5) at any point after 508, when he himself removed sacred vessels from the altar and distributed them for the redemption of captives (*Life* I. 32). If the letter does date to a period before 508, it suggests that the monastery that Caesarius began to build outside the city walls of Arles c.506 was intended to house a small, already existing community of ascetic women led by his sister (*Life* I. 28). The tenor of his advice to this community, with its stern warnings against friendships with young men, elegant clothing, appearances in public, and the dispersal of wealth to wealthy relatives further suggests that it was the kind of household monastery typical of female asceticism at this time. During the war of 507/8, when its unfinished monastery was destroyed and its city threatened with capture, this community may have taken refuge in a monastery in Marseille, from which Caesaria and "two or three companions" could be recalled in 512 to enter the new monastery Caesarius had built for them in a safer location inside the walls (*Life* I. 35).

Although it was soon superseded as a rule for Caesaria's community by the *Regula virginum*, *Letter* 21 long remained popular. Caesaria the Younger quoted parts of it in her letter of 552/7 to Richild and Radegund; a version for men appeared in the seventh century; Defensor of Ligugé cited it on five occasions in his *Liber scintillarum* of c.700; and the council of Aix-la-Chapelle (816) included a long quotation from it.[127]

[126] de Vogüé–Courreau, 39–41.
[127] Ibid., 285–90.

BISHOP CAESARIUS,
LEAST SERVANT OF ALL THE SERVANTS OF GOD,
TO HIS HOLY SISTER ABBESS CAESARIA
AND HER WHOLE CONGREGATION
ETERNAL SALVATION IN CHRIST[128]

1. Venerable daughters in Christ, in presuming in my rustic and unskilled speech to offer you some thoughts on the preservation of quiet and modesty I fear that those who are unaware of the great force of true charity might blame me for presumption. For although I am conscious of my own sins and not unaware of your purity, I presume nonetheless, tepid as I am, to warn the fervent; slow and careless as I am, to spur on those who are moving quickly; weak as I am, to give advice to the healthy; and still on the journey myself, to call you to a longing for the eternal fatherland. And because, in observance of your holy wishes, I am not able to visit you more frequently, I have taken care with perfect charity and pious humility to send to your purity in place of my presence this little pamphlet of advice, in which I have also inserted a few selections from the ancient fathers and have seasoned the aridity of my own style with the pleasantness of, as it were, living fountains. But as I have said, it is charity that knows no fear that thrusts this presumption upon me. And so I ask you, venerable daughters, to pardon my audacity and receive my suggestions patiently and kindly. Out of consideration for my rusticity and modesty reread my exhortation (such as it is) secretly, and do not give it to anyone else, so that the ears of cultivated persons might not be struck by the harshness of my most uncultivated speech. For although we, by the grace of God, perceive nothing wrong with your most sacred way of life, nonetheless, on account of the many snares of the enemy, about whom it is said that he has "a thousand names and a thousand harmful skills,"[129] on account therefore of his poisonous cunning and his deceptively flattering desires, we warn your sacred conscience by these words, lukewarm though they may be. Although an unsuitable warrior

---

[128] This translation is based on the text established by de Vogüé, whose introduction and notes, together with the translation of J. Courreau, have also proved useful, de Vogüé–Courreau, 294–337. A good text of the letter is also available in Morin II, 134–44.
[129] Vergil, *Aen.* VII. 337–8.

myself, I provide spiritual arms for you against the fiery arrows of the
devil.

2. Rejoice therefore and exult in the Lord, venerable daughters, and
constantly give him abundant thanks, for he deigned to attract and to
call you forth from the shadowy life of this world into the tranquil
haven of the religious life. Ponder constantly where you came from and
where you deserved to end up. In faith you left the darkness of the
world and in happiness began to see the light of Christ. You despised
the fire of passion and came to the cool refuge of chastity. You rejected
gluttony and chose abstinence. You rejected avarice and luxury and
took hold of charity and mercy. And although your battle will not be
over until the end of your life, nevertheless, by the grace of God I am
certain of your victory. But I ask you, venerable daughters, to be as
concerned about future matters as you are certain of past ones. For all
crimes and sins quickly return to us, if they are not daily blotted out by
good works. Listen to the apostle Peter who says, "Be sober and keep
watch, because your adversary the devil is going around like a roaring
lion that seeks something to devour" [1 Pet. 5: 8]. For as long as we
live in this body, let us fight back day and night against the devil, with
Christ as our helper and leader. For there are, unfortunately, some heed-
less and tepid people who boast about the mere name of Christianity
and think it sufficient that they have changed their clothing and merely
put on a religious habit. They are ignorant of that saying of a prophet:
"Son, as you enter upon the service of God, stand in justice and fear and
prepare your soul for temptation" [Sir. 2: 1]. Nor do they consider the
psalmist's passage: "For the sake of the words of your lips I have kept
hard ways" [Ps. 17: 4], or what the apostle said: "It is necessary that we
enter the kingdom of heaven through many tribulations" [Acts 14: 22].
For we can take off secular clothing and put on religious habits in the
space of an hour; but we ought to retain a good character and to struggle
against the deceptively sweet pleasures of this world for as long as we
live, with the assistance of Christ.[130] For "not he who has begun, but
he who has persevered to the end will be saved" [Matt. 10: 22].

[130] A paraphrase of Pelagius, *Epist. ad Demetriadem* 24.

3. In the first place, therefore, let every soul that desires to observe a religious way of life struggle with the whole strength of its faith to overcome the desires of gluttony and avoid drunkenness. It should endeavor to have a diet so temperate and a table so moderate that its flesh is not weakened by too much abstinence nor provoked to luxury by an abundance of delights. Then, after rejecting the pride that God resists the soul should lay down the foundations of deep humility.[131] It should detest and flee from envy as it would the venom of a snake; it should check the tongue; it should reject slander as if it were poison. It should neither speak idle words itself nor willingly open its ears to those spoken by another; it should be accustomed to clothing that is neither excessively lowly nor ostentatiously pompous and dangerously elegant; it should frequently read a passage itself or listen to someone else's reading with an avid heart. It should constantly draw the water of salvation from the fountains of divine scripture, that water about which the Lord speaks, "Whoever believes in me, rivers of living water will flow from within him" [John 7: 38]. The holy soul should constantly try to adorn itself with the flowers of paradise, that is, with the contents of the holy scriptures. From these it should uninterruptedly hang precious pearls from its ears. From these it should arrange rings and bracelets by doing good works. There it should seek the remedies for wounds, the spices of chastity, the sacrifices of remorse.

The woman who desires to preserve piety with an immaculate heart and pure body should either never go out in public or only because of great and unavoidable need. She should have contact with men as rarely as possible; as often as it is necessary to see or greet men, however, only those men should be seen who are commended by age and a holy life. But even these men should be seen rarely, as I said, and conversation with them should be not protracted but very brief. Young men should be seen either not at all or only very rarely. Neither laymen nor other religious men should be admitted into incessant familiarity. This is something that not only women should strive to observe concerning men, but also men concerning women, if they wish to protect the complete purity of their chastity. And let no one say, "My conscience is

---

[131] An allusion to Cassian, *Conl.* IX. 3. 2.

sufficient for me."[132] Everyone may tell himself whatever he pleases. But this sort of excuse, which proceeds more from shamelessness than a good conscience, is quite wretched and hateful to God. For when a man makes his first contact with a woman, or a woman with a man, it is recognized as modest enough and even as holy, because at first the devil withdraws his machinations until little by little, as an incessant familiarity grows, "he feeds an inimical friendship between them."[133] For within a short time the cunning devil makes them devoted to one another without any outbreak of passion or loss of chastity. And so he deceives them so completely by a false sense of security that he leads them forth to the sea like two small boats in pleasant tranquillity; and while they think they are safe, they do not seek the help of fasts, which serve as oars, nor of vigils, which act as rudders. When he has made them feel secure, he strikes them against one another and sinks them in a sudden storm. "Forcing them into dangerous embraces, he destroys them together by a single blow. He hides the fire smoldering without any flame until he sets them both aflame at the same time by joining two torches together. Thus the devil loosens what he was seen to preserve before; thus he produces an illicit love from an apparently innocent charity. At first he is content to yield, so that he can take over more later."[134]

Mark this well! Each person is secure about his own conscience in the sense that, when he sees someone, he cannot be scandalized about it. But he does not see the will of another as he knows his own conscience, does he? Indeed, your eye sees another innocently, and perhaps he cruelly lusts after you. Do you rejoice because of your own chastity and not fear the ruin of his? For if you present yourself as too familiar to another, you nourish his lust. Even if you yourself do not sin, you will nevertheless destroy another. And you will be the reason, even without a reason, for another's passion to dishonor you.[135] Do not, I

[132] A reference to Jerome, *Epist.* 22. 13, ed. I. Hilberg, *CSEL* 54 (1910), 160.
[133] Pseudo-Cyprian, *De singularitate clericorum* 19. This treatise was written in the later third century to denounce the practice of cohabitation between clerics and unmarried religious women. Its author is unknown.
[134] Ibid., 19.
[135] A paraphrase of Pseudo-Cyprian, *De singularitate clericorum* 11.

beg you, either provide an occasion to anyone or act in a familiar way, lest perhaps someone's lust for you, once it has been evilly inflamed, might begin to look elsewhere for what it could not find in you.

4. But perhaps a woman says, "I am secure about my own conscience." This statement should not come from the mouth of a religious person, for anyone confident of her own virtue has already fallen. If you desire, with Christ's help, to overcome sexual desire, you ought to avoid intimacy. Anyone who does not shun shameful intimacy should know with utmost certainty that she will quickly destroy either herself or someone else. But perhaps someone says, "I do not avoid intimacy because I want to have what I will conquer, and I desire to hold my adversary captive."[136] See to it that the adversary does not begin to rebel against you. See to it that captivity does not lead you into captivity. Hear the apostle who says, "Avoid fornication" [1 Cor. 6: 18]. We ought to resist the other vices with all our strength. Against sexual desire, however, it is proper not to fight but to flee. Be therefore a fugitive from desire if you wish to be an outstanding warrior for chastity. Diligently pay attention to what I have said. When someone is excited by the tingling of passion while by herself, she should, with Christ's help, fight as much as she can against herself, because she cannot avoid herself. But when the devil supplies an occasion for pleasure through the companionship of another, the holy soul should flee that intimacy, as I said above, to the extent that it can. And so, when someone is tempted in herself, she should resist herself with God's help. When she is stimulated by even the slightest degree of lust through her relationship with another, she should flee it just like a venomous serpent as fast as possible.

5. But so that we might be able to observe all of these instructions, let us maintain a reasonable abstinence, for the saying of that most holy man is true: "To the degree that you curb the stomach, so you also curb its dangerous movements."[137] Let us preserve a true humility to the extent that we can; for the integrity of the flesh is not long preserved when the mind is corrupted by the swelling of pride.

[136] A paraphrase of Pseudo-Cyprian, *De singularitate clericorum* 9, 18.
[137] Rufinus, *Enchiridion Sexti* 240, ed. H. Chadwick, *The Sentences of Sextus* (Cambridge, 1959), 39. See further de Vogüé (1986).

Especially if the flame of anger also rises up frequently, it quickly con-
sumes the flowers of chastity and virginity. Moreover, a chaste soul
and one devoted to God should avoid frequent contact not only with
strangers but even with her own relatives, either when they come to her
or when she goes to them. For [there is a danger] that she will hear
something improper, or say something unfitting, or see something that
can be harmful to chastity. For if the vessels that are offered to the
church to be put on the holy altar are called holy by everyone, and it is
wrong for them to be removed later from the church to the house of a
layman or to be adapted to human uses—if vessels that cannot have either intellect or perception have so much value, what sort of value do
you think a soul created in his image has in God's eyes? Therefore,
just as holy vessels neither can nor ought to be removed from a church
to serve human uses, so it is not proper, suitable, or fitting for any religious person to be entangled in the many obligations of his relations
or to be attached by dangerous familiarity to strangers, whoever they
may be.

6. Of this I warn you above all, to avoid the evil of envy as
though it were the venom of a snake, and to preserve the sweetness of
charity among yourselves so completely that you prepare spiritual
remedies for one another through holy conversation. For there are unfortunately some women who, when they get together, prefer to inflict
wounds by disparaging one another and murmuring against their superi-
ors than to prepare spiritual remedies. But you, holy and venerable
daughters, if you see a woman wavering, give her reassurance; if you
see a woman acting proudly, apply humility as a medicine; if you see
an angry woman, offer her the coolness of patience.

If you were born as noble women, rejoice at the humility of religious life rather than at worldly status. Distribute your earthly wealth
in such a way that you not make carnal shackles by keeping anything
for yourself or by giving it away too late, when you can acquire spiritual wings from it by giving it away well and quickly. For if earthly
wealth is given away too late, it is known to bind the wings of the soul
as if with glue. For what has been written is true: "The impediments

of the world have made them wretched."[138] If anyone was poor before she took up a holy religious way of life, she should thank God for not wishing to bind her to the wealth of this world. For many, unfortunately, are tied down so firmly by their wealth that they cannot return to their eternal homeland. You, however, are now happy even in this life by the favor of Christ, since you have despised wealth together with the pleasures of this world not only in your heart but also in your body. Therefore keep your hands on the plow and do not look back [cf. Luke 9: 62]. And because you have already deserved to climb to the summit of perfection, the pleasures of this world should not displace you from there. "Remember Lot's wife" [Luke 17: 32], who "looked back and was turned into a pillar of salt" [Gen. 19: 26]. A virgin should never swear an oath or utter a curse. Guard not only your bodies but also your hearts with all concern, on account of what has been written: "With closest custody guard your heart" [Prov. 4: 23], and what the Lord said in the gospel: "Evil thoughts come out of the heart" [Matt. 15: 19]. For if nothing evil is thought in your heart, whatever comes forth from your mouth is holy. As it has been written: "The mouth speaks from the abundance of the heart" [Matt. 12: 34]. For the tongue is accustomed to say whatever the conscience has provided from the workshop of the heart. And so if you wish to bring forth good things from your mouth, always think holy thoughts in your heart.

7. You should devote yourselves to reading and prayer in such a way that above all you can also do something with your hands, in accordance with the apostle's saying: "Anyone who does not work should not eat" [2 Thes. 3: 10]. In particular, however, accustom yourselves to make time for reading before the third hour, and dedicate the better part of the day to spiritual works.[139] Let your prayer proceed so silently from your heart that it is scarcely heard in your mouth. For anyone who prays in a loud voice does much harm to herself and others, since through her garrulity she diverts the mind of her neighbor from her holy and secret prayer. In those activities done by hand, despise and scorn pompous and worldly garments, which serve vanity rather than utility, so that even in these earthly activities you can do whatever is

---

[138] *Apocalypse of Paul* 40, ed. M. R. James, *The Apocryphal New Testament* (Oxford, 1924), 546. See further Fischer (1951).
[139] A paraphrase of Pelagius, *Epist. ad Demetriadem* 23.

appropriate to moderation and decency. For many show even in their everyday activities what they value in their way of life. Let those who love the world and are devoted to pleasure and luxury prepare worldly ornaments for themselves. You, however, for whom the world has been crucified, should have nothing in common with these ornaments. You should rather eliminate all garments that outfit the flesh for luxury, since they are hostile to and incompatible with your way of life. For there are unfortunately those who, out of worldly vanity, are more eager to devote their efforts to worldly desires than to spiritual reading, since they wish for the sake of visual pleasure to acquire at huge cost and superfluous expense beautiful carpets, decorated tapestries, embroideries, and the like. They are unaware of the message the Lord proclaims through the evangelist John: "Do not love the world nor the things that are in the world; for everything that is in the world is an enticement of the flesh, an enticement of the eyes, and a worldly display" [1 John 2: 15–16]. What good is it for a virgin to preserve the integrity of her body if she does not wish to avoid the enticements of her eyes?

8. There are also some women who wish to give the greater part of their wealth to relatives—perhaps rich ones at that—rather than to the poor. They do not consider that in distributing their wealth to the former for luxury they are condemning themselves to everlasting poverty. But someone says, "Should I therefore despise my relatives?" Far be it from me to say that you should not honor your relatives. How can I who say that enemies should be loved preach that relatives should not be loved? Love your relatives as much as you can and, if they are chaste and honorable, honor them always and leave them some little gifts from your wealth in memory of yourself. But give the bulk of it, the part that is larger and more useful, to the poor, to be of use until the end of the world. In this way, through the relief of the poor your alms might pass over at Judgment Day to the kingdom of heaven. Your relatives can acquire for themselves later, by working, what you do not give them. But you will never be able to find later what you do not acquire for yourself by way of mercy in this world. Yet if you have any poor relations who do not have sufficient food or clothing, you will receive a reward from God if you give them something capable of supporting them.

For we shall come some day before the tribunal of the eternal Judge; and if we have behaved well, we shall hear to our happiness, "Come blessed ones and receive the kingdom, for I was hungry and thirsty" and so forth [Matt. 25: 34–6], and a little later, "As often as you did it for one of the least of these"—without doubt the poor—"you did it for me" [Matt. 25: 40]. He did not say, "Come and receive the kingdom because you added your wealth to the wealth of your relations, because you gave them the means by which to lead a life of luxury in the world." Certainly he did not say this, but rather what he says in the gospel and what he had said before through the prophet: "He distributed; he gave to the poor" [Ps. 112: 9]. Pay attention, I beg you: "He distributed," he said. "He gave to the poor." He did not say "to the rich," "to the dissolute," or "to those loving this world." For the rich man, about whom we read in the gospel that "he was clothed in purple and linen" [Luke 16: 19], left his brothers rich. But afterwards he sought a drop of refreshment when he was burning in hell, and he could not find one.

But you souls holy and worthy of God, do everything in a spiritual fashion. And to the God to whom you have dedicated your souls, offer—nay return—your wealth. It is right that he who prepares eternal wealth for you receive earthly wealth from you. Let him who conferred the crown of virginity upon you receive earthly wealth from you. Indeed, you are further in debt to him, for he has allowed you to be able to follow him, the unstained lamb, "wherever he goes" [Rev. 14: 4]. The rest of the multitude follows Christ not wherever he goes but as far as they can. Penitents and married women can follow Christ through other paths of righteousness except when he leads the way in the honorable path of virginity. For they do not have the ability to make themselves virgins. But you, holy daughters, follow him by clinging tenaciously to what you ardently vowed.

9. Again and again, holy souls dedicated to God, I ask and humbly presume to advise you that in order to preserve the reward of virginity you work with all your strength to drive irregular intimacy away from yourselves and your souls. May the plague and pestilence that disordered intimacy produces be far enough away from you. "For there is no security in this sort of companionship, which is buffeted as if by

turbulent waves. Friendly harmony does not reside in this intimacy; it produces nothing but disharmonious enmity."[140] The most sacred warrant for preserving the honor of the religious life is solitude rather than an irregular intimacy.

Pay attention, O holy soul, and carefully consider how many evils are born from irregular companionship. For intimacy with anyone, if it begins to be frequent, "does not sow anything except corruption: it engenders vices, conceives desire, gives birth to disgrace, stirs up madness, spreads rage, supports lewdness, nourishes wantonness, produces accidents, erects ruins, overflows banks, opens up steep places, navigates in the midst of dangers, sails in the midst of shipwrecks, rejoices in destruction, fosters death, trades in confusion, treasures up scandal, heaps up crimes, inflames excuses, combines together in a bundle numerous deceitful traps, and through unlimited disgraces leads to many deaths in the destruction of the lost. No one destroys so many and such great evils of dangerous intimacy except she who seldom or almost never seeks a companionship that can endanger her. For if a holy soul wants to preserve its own solitude and flees the evil of constant intimacy with the whole strength of its mind, then holy solitude itself is an unconquered fortification of sacredness for it, a brave assault against infamy, a strengthening of fortitude and a weakening of wanton lewdness, a defense of goodness and a destruction of evil, a victory for the soul and a conquest of the body, a liberation of glory and an enslavement of crimes, a bridesmaid of sanctity and a divorce from turpitude, a proof of sincerity and an elimination of scandals, an exercise of continence and a complete purgation of luxury, a secure peace for virtues and a restless assault against wars, a high point of purity and a prison for lust, a port of honor and a place of shipwreck for dishonor, the mother of virginity and the enemy of filth, a parapet for modesty and a despoiling of shamefulness, a wall of incorruption and a separation from the multitude, the honor of integrity and the condemnation of fornication, the summit of charity and the downfall of shame, a desire for good works and a rejection of vices, a refreshment of modesty and a punishment of wantonness, an acquisition of triumphs and a loss of crimes, a repose of salvation and a destruction of perdition, a life of the spirit and

---

[140] Pseudo-Cyprian, *De singularitate clericorum* 6.

death of the flesh, status of an angelic nature and a death of human substance."[141]

10. With bravery and God's help all these evils are avoided, and the good qualities of which we have spoken are joyfully acquired when holy souls reject irregular intimacy. Pay attention, I beg you, holy souls, for among all the struggles in which the Christian army always takes part only the battles of chastity are more difficult, for there the fighting occurs every day and victory is rare. Chastity has acquired a determined enemy who is daily overcome and daily feared. Daily, I say, he is overcome, and yet he does not cease to challenge us. No one who fights with himself wins a secure victory. Where there are often shipwrecks the sailing is perilous, and it is dangerous to cross in the waves of desire, where many have drowned. For when desire is conquered, it does not end; and though the battles over chastity are fierce, the rewards are greater. The flame that blazes too brightly quickly dies down to ashes; but when you yield to it, the burning of the body is further inflamed rather than ended. No one securely receives the reward of chastity, but the difficulties of someone's struggle are matched by the glory of the result. Whoever takes up a war with nature imposes upon himself a danger worthy of reward. The public enemy spares him at night; the machinations of the brigands attack only in darkness; the desire of passion, however, both provokes him at night and does not spare him by day; nor does it fear the purple garments of kings or shudder at the rags of paupers.

Therefore, so that you can happily receive from a generous God the rewards of chastity and the crown of virginity, always keep dangerous intimacy away from yourselves. Run in faith so that you can arrive in happiness. And be mindful of me when your unstained virginity has been crowned. This letter will provide me with an excuse before Christ's tribunal, for I suggested with true charity and perfect humility what it was fitting for me to say and you to hear. If anyone, God forbid, neglects to obey this letter, it will be a witness against her; whoever willingly accepts it, may she be rewarded with a joy not temporary but permanent. May you prosper in Christ, holy and venerable women.

[141] Closely adapted from pseudo-Cyprian, *De singularitate clericorum* 38–9.

SELECT BIBLIOGRAPHY

CAESARIUS OF ARLES

The starting place is Morin I and II, which includes
Caesarius's own corpus as well as other documents relevant to his career. Apart from his *Life*, *Testament*, and *Letters*, this corpus consists
of sermons, monastic rules, theological treatises, church councils, and
other documents relating to his monastery.

Caesarius's *Sermones* are available in Morin I, and reprinted in
CCSL 103–104 (1953). They are also included on the *Cetedoc Library
of Christian Latin Texts*, a CD-ROM published by Brepols in 1991.
An English translation of the *Sermones* can be found in M. M.
Mueller, *Caesarius of Arles. Sermons*, 3 vols., The Fathers of the
Church 31, 47, and 66 (Washington, D.C., 1956–73). A more recent
edition of *Sermones* 1–80, with an excellent introduction and French
translation, is available in Delage (1971–86). For a list of sermons
discovered since the publication of Morin's edition, see Klingshirn
(1993), 288.

Caesarius's *Regula virginum* is edited in Morin II, 99–124,
and de Vogüé–Courreau, 35–273. An English translation with introduction and notes can be found in M. C. McCarthy, *The Rule for Nuns
of St. Caesarius of Arles*, The Catholic University of America Studies
in Mediaeval History, n.s. 16 (Washington, D.C., 1960). His *Regula
monachorum* is edited in Morin II, 149–55. The theological treatises
plausibly attributed to Caesarius by Morin include the *De gratia* (Morin
II, 159–64), *De mysterio trinitatis* (Morin II, 164–80), *Breviarium
adversus hereticos* (Morin II, 180–208), and *Expositio in Apocalypsim*
(Morin II, 209–77).

Latin texts of the canons of Caesarius's church councils can be
found in Morin II, 35–89, as well as in *Concilia Galliae, A. 314–A.
506*, and *Concilia Galliae, A. 511–A. 695*. A close English paraphrase
of their canons, with commentary, is available in K. J. Hefele, *A
History of the Councils of the Church*, trans. W. R. Clark, 5 vols.
(Edinburgh, 1883–96, repr. New York, 1972). A French translation of
the fourth-century councils with introduction and notes can be found in
Conciles gaulois du IVe siècle, ed. J. Gaudemet, *SC* 241 (1977);
canons of the sixth- and seventh-century councils appear in *Les Canons
des conciles mérovingiens (VIe–VIIe siècles)*, ed J. Gaudemet and B.

Basdevant, *SC* 353–354 (1989); the fifth-century councils including Agde (506) will appear in a forthcoming volume of *SC*.
    A select annotated bibliography of work about Caesarius to 1963 can be found in G. Terraneo, "Saggio bibliografico su Cesario vescovo di Arles," *La scuola cattolica* 91 (1963), Suppl. bibliogr. 272*–94*. Current bibliography is regularly published in *Medioevo Latino*, *Revue d' histoire ecclésiastique*, and *L'Année philologique*.

ANCIENT SOURCES

Ancient sources cited more than once are listed here. Texts referred to only once are cited in full in the notes where they appear. Place of publication is not given for works published in *CCSL, CSEL, MGH, PL*, or *SC*. Classical texts not listed here are available in the *Loeb Classical Library*. Translations are listed where available. Translations cited by author and date in the introduction and notes are listed in the bibliography of secondary works.

Avitus of Vienne. *Epistulae ad diversos*. Ed. R. Peiper. *MGH AA* 6. 2 (1883), 35–103.
Cassian. *Conlationes*. Ed. M. Petschenig. *CSEL* 13 (1886). Trans. E. C. S. Gibson, *NPNF*, 2nd ser., 11 (1894), 291–545.
Cassian. *De institutis coenobiorum*. Ed. M. Petschenig. CSEL 17 (1888). Trans. E. C. S. Gibson, *NPNF*, 2nd ser., 11 (1894), 201–90.
Concilia Galliae, A. 314–A. 506. Ed. C. Munier. *CCSL* 148 (1963).
Concilia Galliae, A. 511–A. 696. Ed. C. de Clercq. *CCSL* 148A (1963).
Decrees of the Ecumenical Councils. Ed. N. P. Tanner. I. London and Washington, D.C., 1990.
Ennodius. *Epistulae*. Ed. G. Hartel. *CSEL* 6 (1882), 1–260.
Ennodius. *Vita Epiphani*. Ed. F. Vogel. *MGH AA* 7 (1885), 84–109. Trans. G. M. Cook. *The Life of Saint Epiphanius*. The Catholic University of America Studies in Medieval and Renaissance Language and Literature 14. Washington, D. C., 1942.
Epistulae Arelatenses. Ed. W. Gundlach. *MGH Ep*. 3 (1892), 1–83.

Gregory of Tours. *In Gloria confessorum*. Ed. B. Krusch. *MGH SRM* 1. 2 (1885), 294–370. Trans. R. Van Dam. *Gregory of Tours: Glory of the Confessors*. *TTH* 4. Liverpool, 1988.

Gregory of Tours. *Historiae*. Ed. B. Krusch and W. Levison. 2nd ed. *MGH SRM* 1. 1 (1937–51). Trans. Dalton (1927) II.

Hilarius of Arles. *Vita Honorati*. Ed. Cavallin (1952), 48–78. Trans. Hoare (1954), 247–80.

Liber pontificalis. Ed. L. Duchesne. *Le Liber Pontificalis*. 2nd ed. 3 vols. Paris, 1955–7. Trans. R. Davis. *The Book of Pontiffs (Liber Pontificalis to AD 715)*. *TTH* 6. Liverpool, 1989.

Pelagius. *Epistula ad Demetriadem*. *PL* 30: 13–45.

Julianus Pomerius. *De vita contemplativa*. *PL* 59: 411–520. Trans. Suelzer (1947).

Possidius. *Vita Augustini*. Ed. H. T. Weiskotten. *Sancti Augustini Vita Scripta a Possidio Episcopo*. Princeton, 1919. Trans. Hoare (1954), 191–244.

Procopius. *De bellis*. Ed. J. Haury and G. Wirth. 2 vols. Leipzig, 1962–3. Trans. H. B. Dewing. *Loeb Classical Library*. 5 vols. London and Cambridge, Mass., 1914–28.

Pseudo-Cyprian. *De singularitate clericorum*. Ed. G. Hartel. *CSEL* 3. 3 (1871), 173–220.

Regula Benedicti. Ed. T. Fry. *RB 1980: The Rule of St. Benedict in Latin and English with Notes*. Collegeville, Minn., 1981.

Regula Macarii. Ed. de Vogüé (1982), 372–88. Trans. C. V. Franklin, I. Havener, and J. A. Francis. *Early Monastic Rules*. Collegeville, Minn., 1982.

Ruricius of Limoges. *Epistulae*. Ed. A. Engelbrecht. *CSEL* 21 (1891), 349–442.

Sidonius Apollinaris. *Epistulae*. Ed. C. Luetjohann. *MGH AA* 8 (1887), 1–172. Trans. W. B. Anderson. *Loeb Classical Library*. 2 vols. London and Cambridge, Mass., 1936–65.

Statuta ecclesiae antiqua. Ed. C. Munier. *Les Statuta Ecclesiae Antiqua*. Paris, 1960.

Sulpicius Severus. *Vita Martini*. Ed. C. Halm. CSEL 1 (1866), 107–37. Trans. Hoare (1954), 3–44.

Sulpicius Severus. *Dialogi*. Ed. C. Halm. *CSEL* 1 (1866), 152–216. Trans. Hoare (1954), 63–144.

Valentinian. *Novellae*. Ed. T. Mommsen and P. M. Meyer. *Theodosiani Libri XVI*. 2nd ed. II. Berlin, 1954, 69–154. Trans. C. Pharr. *The Theodosian Code and Novels and the Sirmondian Constitutions*. Princeton, 1952, 515–50.

Vita Hilarii. Ed. Cavallin (1952), 80–109.

SECONDARY WORKS

This list includes all works cited by author and date as well as selected additional bibliography on Caesarius.

d'Achery, L. and J. Mabillon, eds. (1668). *Acta Sanctorum Ordinis Sancti Benedicti*. I. Paris, 1668. Repr. Mâcon, 1935.

Arbesmann, R. (1979). "The 'cervuli' and 'anniculae' in Caesarius of Arles." *Traditio* 35 (1979), 89–119.

Arnold, C. F. (1894). *Caesarius von Arelate und die gallische Kirche seiner Zeit*. Leipzig, 1894.

Auerbach, E. (1965). *Literary Language and its Public in Late Latin Antiquity and in the Middle Ages*. Trans. R. Manheim. London, 1965.

Bagnall, R. S. et al. (1987). *Consuls of the Later Roman Empire*. Atlanta, Ga., 1987.

Bambeck, M. (1983). "Fischer und Bauern gegen Philosophen und sonstige Großkopfeten—ein christlicher 'Topos' in Antike und Mittelalter." *Mittellateinisches Jahrbuch* 18 (1983), 29–50.

Barruol, G. (1969). *Les Peuples préromains du Sud-Est de la Gaule*. Revue archéologique de Narbonnaise. Suppl. 1. Paris, 1969.

Beck, H.-G. (1980). "The Henoticon and the Acacian Schism." In *History of the Church*, ed. H. Jedin and J. Dolan. II: *The Imperial Church from Constantine to the Early Middle Ages*. Ed. K. Baus et al. Trans. A. Biggs. New York, 1980, 421–33.

Beck, H. G. J. (1950). *The Pastoral Care of Souls in South-East France During the Sixth Century*. Rome, 1950.

Bedard, W. M. (1951). *The Symbolism of the Baptismal Font in Early Christian Thought*. The Catholic University of America Studies in Sacred Theology, 2nd ser., 45. Washington, D. C., 1951.

Benoit, F. (1935). *Les cimetières suburbains d'Arles dans l'Antiquité chrétienne et au Moyen Age*. Rome, 1935.

Benoit, F. (1936). *Forma Orbis Romani: Carte archéologique de la Gaule romaine.* V. Paris, 1936.

Benoit, F. (1951). "Le premier baptistère d'Arles et l'abbaye Saint-Césaire." *Cahiers archéologiques* 5 (1951), 31–59.

Biarne, J. (1981). "Le temps du moine d'après les premières règles monastiques d'Occident (IV–VIe siècles)." In *Le Temps chrétien de la fin de l'Antiquité au Moyen Age–IIIe–XIIIe siècles.* Paris, 1981, 99–128.

Bieler, L. (1937). "Zur Mosella des Ausonius: 'cliens' in der Bedeutung 'colonus'." *Rheinisches Museum* 86 (1937), 285–7.

Blumenkranz, B. (1949). "Die Juden als Zeugen der Kirche." *Theologische Zeitschrift* 5 (1949), 396–8.

Boglioni, P. (1979). "La scène de la mort dans les premières hagiographies latines." In *Le Sentiment de la mort au moyen âge,* ed. C. Sutto. Montréal, 1979, 185–210.

Bonner, C. (1932). "Demons of the Bath." In *Studies Presented to F. Ll. Griffith.* London, 1932, 203–8.

Braun, J. (1907). *Die liturgische Gewandung.* Freiburg-im-Breisgau, 1907.

Brennan, B. (1985). "'Episcopae': Bishops' Wives Viewed in Sixth-Century Gaul." *Church History* 54 (1985), 311–23.

Brown, P. (1981). *The Cult of the Saints: Its Rise and Function in Latin Christianity.* Chicago, 1981.

Brown, P. (1988). *The Body and Society: Men, Women, and Sexual Renunciation in Early Christianity.* New York, 1988.

Burckhardt, M. (1938). *Die Briefsammlung des Bischofs Avitus von Vienne (†518).* Berlin, 1938.

Burns, J. P., trans. and ed. (1981). *Theological Anthropology.* Philadelphia, 1981.

Carruthers, M. J. (1990). *The Book of Memory: A Study of Memory in Medieval Culture.* Cambridge, 1990.

Caspar, E. (1930–3). *Geschichte des Papsttums.* 2 vols. Tübingen, 1930–3.

Cavallin, S. (1934). *Literarhistorische und textkritische Studien zur Vita S. Caesarii Arelatensis.* Lund, 1934.

Cavallin, S. (1935–6). "Eine neue Handschrift der Vita S. Caesarii Arelatensis." *Kungl. Humanistiska Vetenskapssamfundet i Lund,*

Årsberättelse = *Bulletin de la Société Royale des Lettres de Lund* (1935–6), 9–19.

Cavallin, S. (1948). "Les clausules des hagiographes arlésiens." *Eranos* 46 (1948), 133–57.

Cavallin, S., ed. (1952). *Vitae Sanctorum Honorati et Hilarii.* Lund, 1952.

Claude, D. (1963). "Die Bestellung der Bischöfe im merowingischen Reiche." *Zeitschrift der Savigny-Stiftung für Rechtsgeschichte,* Kan. Abt., 49 (1963), 1–75.

Collins, R. (1983). "Theodebert I, 'Rex Magnus Francorum'." In *Ideal and Reality in Frankish and Anglo-Saxon Society,* ed. P. Wormald. Oxford, 1983, 7–33.

Dalton, O. M. (1927). *The History of the Franks by Gregory of Tours.* I: *Introduction.* II: *Text.* Oxford, 1927.

Daly, W. M. (1970). "Caesarius of Arles. A Precursor of Medieval Christendom." *Traditio* 26 (1970), 1–28.

Delage, M.-J., ed. (1971–86). *Césaire d'Arles. Sermons au Peuple.* 3 vols. *SC* 175, 243, 330. Paris, 1971–86.

Dubois, A. (1903). *La Latinité d'Ennodius.* Paris, 1903.

Etaix, R. (1975). "Trois notes sur saint Césaire d'Arles." In *Corona Gratiarum: Miscellanea Patristica, Historica et Liturgica Eligio Dekkers O. S. B. XII Lustra Complenti Oblata.* I. Brugge, 1975, 211–27.

Ewig, E. (1979). "Beobachtungen zu den Klosterprivilegien des 7. und frühen 8. Jahrhunderts." In his *Spätantikes und fränkisches Gallien. Gesammelte Schriften (1952–1973),* ed. H. Atsma. II. Munich, 1979, 411–26.

Février, P.-A. (1964). *Le Développement urbain en Provence de l'époque romaine à la fin du XIVᵉ siècle.* Paris, 1964.

Février, P.-A. (1986a). "Arles." In *Topographie chrétienne des cités de la Gaule,* ed. N. Gauthier and J.-Ch. Picard. III: *Provinces ecclésiastiques de Vienne et d'Arles.* Paris, 1986, 73–84.

Février, P.-A. (1986b). "Orange." In *Topographie chrétienne des cités de la Gaule,* ed. N. Gauthier and J.-Ch. Picard. III: *Provinces ecclésiastiques de Vienne et d'Arles.* Paris, 1986, 95–9.

Fischer, B. (1951). "Impedimenta Mundi Fecerunt Eos Miseros." *Vigiliae Christianae* 5 (1951), 84–7.

Fixot, M. (1986). "Les inhumations privilegiées en Provence." In *L'Inhumation privilegiée du IVe au VIIIe siècle en Occident*, ed. Y. Duval and J.-Ch. Picard. Paris, 1986, 117–28.

Flint, V. I. J. (1991). *The Rise of Magic in Early Medieval Europe.* Princeton, 1991.

Fontaine, J. (1962). "Ennodius." *Reallexikon für Antike und Christentum* V (Stuttgart, 1962), cols. 399–421.

Fusconi, G. M. (1963). "Cipriano." *Bibliotheca Sanctorum* III (Rome, 1963), cols. 1280–1.

Goelzer, H. and A. Mey (1909). *Le Latin de Saint Avit.* Paris, 1909.

Goffart, W. (1974). *Caput and Colonate.* Toronto, 1974.

Griffe, E. (1964–6). *La Gaule chrétienne à l'époque romaine.* 2nd ed. 3 vols. Paris, 1964–6.

Griffe, E. (1980). "L'idéal pastoral selon Saint Césaire d'Arles." *Bulletin de littérature ecclésiastique* 81 (1980), 50–4.

Hagendahl, H. (1952). *La Correspondance de Ruricius.* Göteborg, 1952.

Heinzelmann, M. (1982). "Gallische Prosopographie, 260–527." *Francia* 10 (1982), 531–718.

Hillgarth, J. N., ed. (1986). *Christianity and Paganism, 350–750.* Philadelphia, 1986.

Hoare, F. R. (1954). *The Western Fathers.* London, 1954.

Hubert, J. (1947). "La topographie religieuse d'Arles au VIe siècle." *Cahiers archéologiques* 2 (1947), 17–27.

Isetta, S. (1983). "Rassegna di studi Avitani (1857–1982)." *Bollettino di studi latini* 13 (1983), 59–73.

James, E. (1982). *The Origins of France: From Clovis to the Capetians, 500–1000.* London, 1982.

James, E. (1988). *The Franks.* Oxford, 1988.

Janson, T. (1964). *Latin Prose Prefaces: Studies in Literary Conventions.* Stockholm, 1964.

Jay, P. (1957). "Le purgatoire dans la prédication de saint Césaire d'Arles." *Recherches de Théologie ancienne et médiévale* 24 (1957), 5–14.

Jones, A. H. M. (1964). *The Later Roman Empire.* 3 vols. Oxford, 1964. Repr. Baltimore, Md., 1986.

Jones, A. H. M., P. Grierson, and J. A. Crook (1957). "The Authenticity of the 'Testamentum S. Remigii'." *Revue Belge de philologie et d'histoire* 35 (1957), 356–73.

Juster, J. (1914). *Les Juifs dans l'empire romain*. 2 vols. Paris, 1914.

Klingshirn, W. (1985). "Charity and Power: Caesarius of Arles and the Ransoming of Captives in Sub-Roman Gaul." *Journal of Roman Studies* 75 (1985), 183–203.

Klingshirn, W. E. (1990). "Caesarius's Monastery for Women in Arles and the Composition and Function of the 'Vita Caesarii'." *Revue Bénédictine* 100 (1990), 441–81.

Klingshirn, W. E. (1992). "Church Politics and Chronology: Dating the Episcopacy of Caesarius of Arles." *Revue des Etudes Augustiniennes* 38 (1992), 80–8.

Klingshirn, W. E. (1994). *Caesarius of Arles: The Making of a Christian Community in Late Antique Gaul*. Cambridge, 1993.

Ladner, G. (1959). *The Idea of Reform*. Cambridge, Mass., 1959.

Lesne, E. (1910–43). *Histoire de la Proprieté ecclésiastique en France*. 6 vols. Lille, 1910–43.

Lévi, I. (1895). "Saint Césaire et les Juifs d'Arles." *Revue des études juives* 30 (1895), 295–8.

Löfstedt, E. (1950). *Coniectanea: Untersuchungen auf dem Gebiete der antiken und mittelalterlichen Latinität*. Uppsala and Stockholm, 1950.

Loyen, A., ed. (1960). *Sidoine Apollinaire*. I: *Poèmes*. Paris, 1960.

MacCormack, S. (1981). *Art and Ceremony in Late Antiquity*. Berkeley and Los Angeles, 1981.

McCready, W. D. (1989). *Signs of Sanctity: Miracles in the Thought of Gregory the Great*. Toronto, 1989.

McKitterick, R. (1977). *The Frankish Church and the Carolingian Reforms, 789–895*. London, 1977.

McLaughlin, T. P. (1935). *Le Très Ancien Droit monastique de l'Occident*. Paris, 1935.

Malnory, A. (1894). *Saint Césaire, évêque d'Arles*. Bibliothèque de l'école des hautes études 103. Paris, 1894. Repr. Geneva, 1978.

Markus, R. A. (1989). "The Legacy of Pelagius: Orthodoxy, Heresy, and Conciliation." In *The Making of orthodoxy: Essays in honour of Henry Chadwick*, ed. R. Williams. Cambridge, 1989, 214–34.

Mathisen, R. W. (1981). "Epistolography, Literary Circles and Family Ties in Later Roman Gaul." *Transactions of the American Philological Association* 111 (1981), 95–109.

Mathisen, R. (1989). *Ecclesiastical Factionalism and Religious Controversy in Fifth-Century Gaul.* Washington, D.C., 1989.

Matthews, J. F. (1974). "The Letters of Symmachus." In *Latin Literature of the Fourth Century*, ed. J. W. Binns. London, 1974, 58–99.

Meslin, M. (1970). *La fête des kalendes de Janvier dans l'empire romain.* Collection Latomus 115. Brussels, 1970.

Miller, T. S. (1985). *The Birth of the Hospital in the Byzantine Empire.* Baltimore, Md., 1985.

Moorhead, J. (1992). *Theoderic in Italy.* Oxford, 1992.

Morin, G. (1899). "Le testament de S. Césaire d'Arles et la critique de M. Bruno Krusch." *Revue Bénédictine* 16 (1899), 97–112.

Morin, G. (1935). "Maximien évêque de Trèves dans une lettre d'Avit de Vienne." *Revue Bénédictine* 47 (1935), 207–11.

Nicholas, B. (1962). *An Introduction to Roman Law.* Oxford, 1962.

Nonn, U. (1972). "Merowingische Testamente: Studien zum Fortleben einer römischen Urkundenform im Frankenreich." *Archiv für Diplomatik* 18 (1972), 1–129.

Norberg, D. (1968). *Manuel pratique de latin médiéval.* Paris, 1968.

O'Brien, M. B. (1930). *Titles of Address in Christian Latin Epistolography to 543 A.D.* The Catholic University of America Patristic Studies 21. Washington, D. C., 1930.

O'Donnell, J. (1981). "Liberius the Patrician." *Traditio* 37 (1981), 31–72.

Payer, P. J. (1980). "Early medieval regulations concerning marital sexual relations." *Journal of Medieval History* 6 (1980), 353–76.

Plumpe, J. C. (1943). *Mater Ecclesia.* The Catholic University of America Studies in Christian Antiquity 5. Washington, D. C., 1943.

Poly, J.-P. (1976). *La Provence et la société féodale (879–1166).* Paris, 1976.

Posner, E. (1972). *Archives in the Ancient World.* Cambridge, Mass., 1972.

Pricoco, S. (1978). *L'isola dei santi. Il cenobio di Lerino e le origini del monachesimo gallico.* Rome, 1978.

Richards, J. (1979). *The Popes and the Papacy in the Early Middle Ages, 476–752*. London, 1979.

Rivet, A. L. F. (1988). *Gallia Narbonensis: Southern Gaul in Roman Times*. London, 1988.

Rosenberg, H. (1982). "Bishop Avitus of Vienne and the Burgundian Kingdom, A.D. 494–518." *Journal of the Rocky Mountain Medieval and Renaissance Association* 3 (1982), 1–12.

Rostaing, C. (1950). *Essai sur la toponymie de la Provence*. Paris, 1950.

Rouche, M. (1987). "The Early Middle Ages in the West." In *A History of Private Life*, ed. P. Ariès and G. Duby. I: *From Pagan Rome to Byzantium*. Ed. P. Veyne. Trans. A. Goldhammer. Cambridge, Mass., 1987, 411–547.

Schäferdiek, K. (1967). *Die Kirche in den Reichen der Westgoten und Suewen bis zur Errichtung der westgotischen katholischen Staatskirche*. Berlin, 1967.

Scheibelreiter, G. (1983). "Der frühfränkische Episkopat: Bild und Wirklichkeit." *Frühmittelalterliche Studien* 17 (1983), 131–47.

Scheibelreiter, G. (1984). "The Death of the Bishop in the Early Middle Ages." In *The End of Strife*, ed. D. Loades. Edinburgh, 1984, 32–43.

Schneider, J. (1954). "Brief." *Reallexikon für Antike und Christentum* II (Stuttgart, 1954), cols. 564–85.

Solignac, A. (1974). "Julien Pomère." *Dictionnaire de Spiritualité* VIII (Paris, 1974), cols. 1594–1600.

Sticca, G. (1954). "La biografia di Cesario vescovo di Arles, 470–549." Tesi di Laurea, University of Turin, 1954.

Strunk, G. (1970). *Kunst und Glaube in der lateinischen Heiligenlegende*. Munich, 1970.

Suelzer, M. J., ed. (1947). *Julianus Pomerius. The Contemplative Life*. Westminster, Md., 1947.

Van Dam, R. (1985). *Leadership and Community in Late Antique Gaul*. Berkeley and Los Angeles, 1985.

Viard, P. (1964). "Firmino." *Bibliotheca Sanctorum* V (Rome, 1964), cols. 872–3.

Vogt, H. J. "Theological Discussions." In *History of the Church*, ed. H. Jedin and J. Dolan. II: *The Imperial Church from Constantine to the Early Middle Ages.* Ed. K. Baus et al. Trans. A. Biggs. New York, 1980, 707–35.

de Vogüé, A. (1982). *Règles des saints pères.* 2 vols. *SC* 297–298. Paris, 1982.

de Vogüé, A. (1986). "Deux Sentences de Sextus dans les oeuvres de Césaire d'Arles." *Sacris Erudiri* 29 (1986), 19–24.

Wallace-Hadrill, J. M. (1983). *The Frankish Church.* Oxford, 1983.

Wemple, S. F. (1981). *Women in Frankish Society. Marriage and the Cloister, 500–900.* Philadelphia, 1981.

Wilken, R. (1990). "Monophysitism." *Encyclopedia of Early Christianity,* ed. E. Ferguson. New York and London, 1990, 620–2.

Wilmart, A. (1909). "Les *Monita* de l'abbé Porcaire." *Revue Bénédictine* 26 (1909), 475-80.

Wolfram, H. (1988). *History of the Goths.* Trans. T. J. Dunlap. Berkeley and Los Angeles, 1988.

Wood, I. N. (1980). "Avitus of Vienne: Religion and Culture in the Auvergne and the Rhône Valley, 470–530." D. Phil. thesis, Oxford, 1980.

Wood, I. N. (1985). "Gregory of Tours and Clovis." *Revue Belge de philologie et d'histoire* 63 (1985), 249–72.

INDEX

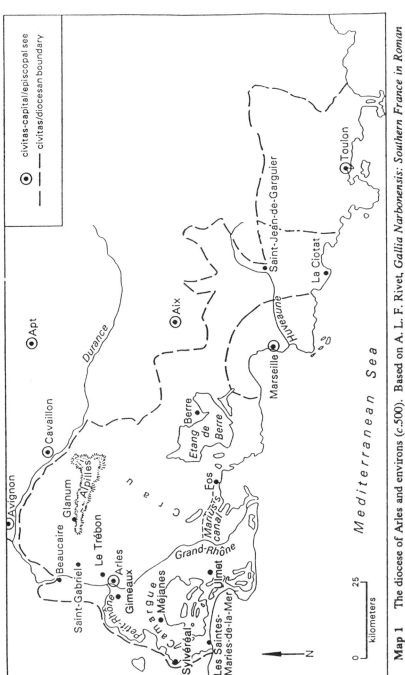

Map 1 The diocese of Arles and environs (c.500). Based on A. L. F. Rivet, *Gallia Narbonensis: Southern France in Roman Times* (London: B. T. Batsford, Ltd., 1988), 204, and M. Chalon and M. Gayraud, "Notes de géographie antique, II," *Revue archéologique de Narbonnaise* 15 (1982), 403.

Legend:
- civitas-capital/episcopal see
- — — — civitas/diocesan boundary

Avignon
Beaucaire
Saint-Gabriel
Glanum
Alpilles
Le Trébon
Arles
Gimeaux
Petit-Rhône
Camargue
Méjanes
Sylvéréal
Les Saintes-Maries-de-la-Mer
Ulmet
Grand-Rhône
Crau
Marius's canal
Fos
Etang de Berre
Berre
Cavaillon
Durance
Apt
Aix
Marseille
Huveaune
Saint-Jean-de-Garguier
La Ciotat
Toulon
Mediterranean Sea
N
0 25
kilometers

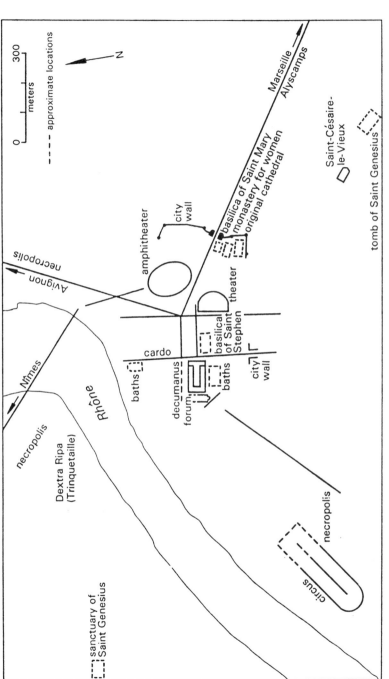

Map 2 The city and suburbs of Arles (c.530). Based on C. Sintès, "L'évolution topographique de l'Arles du Haut-Empire à la lumière des fouilles récentes," *Journal of Roman Archaeology* 5 (1992), 134, and *Topographie chrétienne des cités de la Gaule*, ed. N. Gauthier and J.-Ch. Picard, III: *Provinces ecclésiastiques de Vienne et d'Arles* (Paris: de Boccard, 1986), 75.

Labels within the map:

0 — 300 meters
N
- - - - approximate locations

necropolis
Avignon
Nîmes
Rhône
Dextra Ripa (Trinquetaille)
necropolis
sanctuary of Saint Genesius
amphitheater
city wall
baths
cardo
decumanus
forum
baths
theater
basilica of Saint Stephen
city wall
basilica of Saint Mary
monastery for women
original cathedral
Marseille
Alyscamps
Saint-Césaire-le-Vieux
tomb of Saint Genesius
necropolis
circus

TRANSLATED TEXTS FOR HISTORIANS
Published Titles

Gregory of Tours: Life of the Fathers
Translated with an introduction by EDWARD JAMES
Volume 1: 176pp., 2nd edition 1991, ISBN 0 85323 327 6

The Emperor Julian: Panegyric and Polemic
Claudius Mamertinus, John Chrysostom, Ephrem the Syrian
edited by SAMUEL N. C. LIEU
Volume 2: 153pp., 2nd edition 1989, ISBN 0 85323 376 4

Pacatus: Panegyric to the Emperor Theodosius
Translated with an introduction by C. E. V. NIXON
Volume 3: 122pp., 1987, ISBN 0 85323 076 5

Gregory of Tours: Glory of the Martyrs
Translated with an introduction by RAYMOND VAN DAM
Volume 4: 150pp., 1988, ISBN 0 85323 236 9

Gregory of Tours: Glory of the Confessors
Translated with an introduction by RAYMOND VAN DAM
Volume 5: 127pp., 1988, ISBN 0 85323 226 1

The Book of Pontiffs (*Liber Pontificalis to AD 715*)
Translated with an introduction by RAYMOND DAVIS
Volume 6: 175pp., 1989, ISBN 0 85323 216 4

Chronicon Paschale 284-628 AD
Translated with notes and introduction by
MICHAEL WHITBY AND MARY WHITBY
Volume 7: 280pp., 1989, ISBN 0 85323 096 X

Iamblichus: On the Pythagorean Life
Translated with notes and introduction by GILLIAN CLARK
Volume 8: 144pp., 1989, ISBN 0 85323 326 8

Conquerors and Chroniclers of Early-Medieval Spain
Translated with notes and introduction by KENNETH BAXTER WOLF
Volume 9: 176pp., 1991, ISBN 0 85323 047 1

Victor of Vita: History of the Vandal Persecution
Translated with notes and introduction by JOHN MOORHEAD
Volume 10: 112pp., 1992, ISBN 0 85323 127 3

The Goths in the Fourth Century
by PETER HEATHER AND JOHN MATTHEWS
Volume 11: 224pp., 1991, ISBN 0 85323 426 4

Cassiodorus: *Variae*
Translated with notes and introduction by S.J.B. BARNISH
Volume 12: 260pp., 1992, ISBN 0 85323 436 1

The Lives of the Eighth-Century Popes (*Liber Pontificalis*)
Translated with an introduction and commentary by RAYMOND DAVIS
Volume 13: 288pp., 1992, ISBN 0 85323 018 8